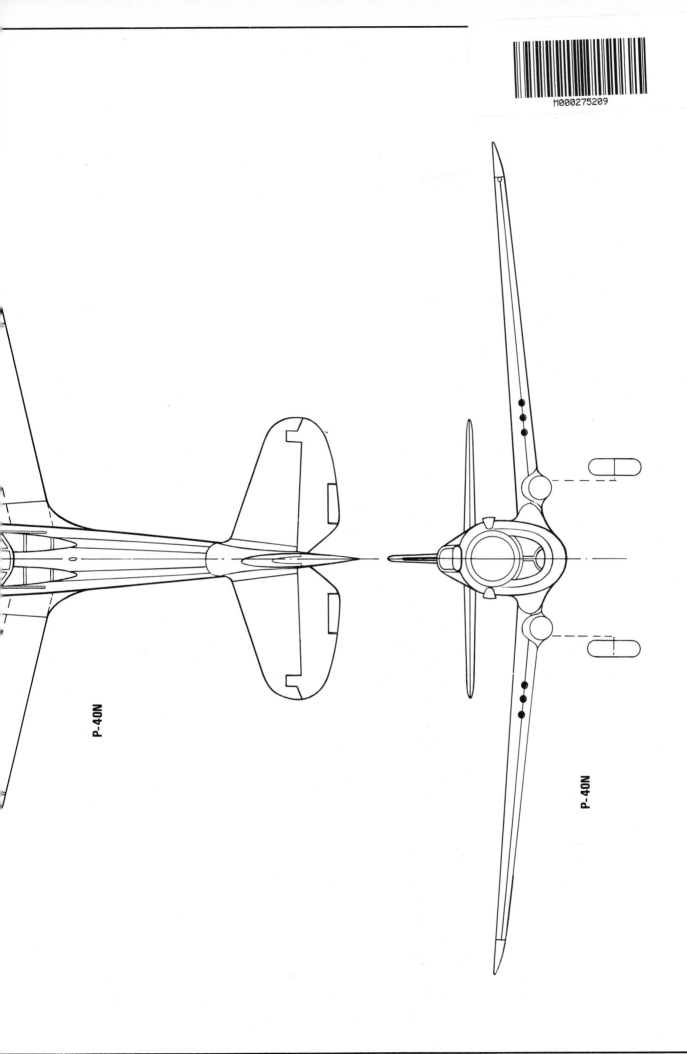

P-40N

P-40N

P-40 HAWKS
AT WAR

P-40 HAWKS
AT WAR

Joe Christy & Jeff Ethell

Charles Scribner's Sons
NEW YORK

Acknowledgments

The authors are indebted to the following people who, with unfailing patience and good humour in honouring our requests for help, made this book possible:

From the USAF Office of Information, Maj Pete Hefler and Capt Rick DuCharme; USAF AAVS, Mrs Ginny Fincik (as always!); fellow researchers Christopher Shores, Mike Minnich and Evan Hull; those very knowledgeable Australians, Frank F. Smith and T. R. Bennett; Bruce Hoy of the Air Museum, Papua, New Guinea; author/historian Ernest McDowell; ex-Flying Tigers C. H. 'Link' Laughlin and R. T. Smith, P-40 crew chief Henry J. Straub; P-40 commanders and pilots Gen Ben Kelsey, Gen Ben O. Davis, Jr, Archie Knight, Don Lopez, Joseph H. Moore, Pancho Pasqualicio, Harry Brown, Clive Caldwell, Don Taylor, Charlie Cook and the late William Stubbs, along with P-36/P-40 designer Dr Donovan R. Berlin. Our thanks are also owed to the nice people at the Air Force Museum, Wright-Patterson AFB, and to old hand Lou Casey, National Air & Space Museum, Washington, DC.

Joe Christy and Jeff Ethell

First U.S. edition published by
Charles Scribner's Sons 1980

Copyright under the Berne Convention

All rights reserved. No part of this book
may be reproduced in any form without the
permission of Charles Scribner's Sons

1 3 5 7 9 11 13 15 17 19 I/C 20 18 16 14 12 10 8 6 4 2

Printed in Great Britain

Library of Congress Catalog Card Number 79-89277
ISBN: 0-684-16441-8

Contents

Preface

The question as to which fighter aeroplane of World War II was the 'best' requires so many qualifiers it becomes irrelevant. A more useful determination would be which fighter was the most important, although that, too, demands its qualifiers. Obviously, the most important aircraft were whatever we happened to have at a given time and place; the ones that were 'there' at a critical time.

Especially important were the machines that carried the burden during the most desperate days when the outcome of that global conflict was still in doubt; and one of those was the Curtiss P-40, known to the British and Commonwealth Nations as the Tomahawk and Kittyhawk. This fighter, or its parent, the P-36 Mohawk, was in service throughout the war, and in almost all the theatres of operations, and the measure of its importance – easily obscured by spectacular performances of newer designs after victory was assured – may be fairly taken only when we examine the conditions under which it fought.

Still, it was simply a machine, a weapon. As with all other weapons of freedom, the P-40's importance was determined by the men who took her into battle. Therefore, if the P-40 story is primarily a story about people, we at least need no qualifiers when we state that these were among the best.

1 The Hawk Family Tree

Had not John K. Northrop of the Northrop Aircraft Corporation and his chief engineer, Dr Donovan R. Berlin, heatedly disagreed over the wing design of a new Northrop fighter in June, 1934, at least one, and perhaps two of World War II's most historic fighter aeroplanes – the P-40 and P-51 – would never have appeared.

But these men did disagree, and when Don Berlin adamantly insisted that the new Northrop wing would be subject to flutter, Northrop fired him.

That resulted in Berlin going to work for Curtiss-Wright; which in turn resulted in the Berlin-designed P-36 Hawk, which eventually furnished its airframe to more than 13,000 Tomahawks, Kittyhawks and Warhawks that followed.

The P-51? Well, we'll come to that momentarily. That is a part of the Hawk story that must be carefully presented, because it shoots down a long-standing fiction about the Mustang's origin and its miraculous 120-day gestation period.

The aircraft that the US Army Air Corps would later call the P-36 was simply Curtiss Design No 75 when Don Berlin began work on it in October 1934. It was intended for an Army fighter competition scheduled for the following May, and hopefully would re-establish Curtiss as a major producer of American fighter aircraft. The Army Air Corps had not placed an order for Curtiss fighters since 1931, and during the Great Depression of the early 1930s Curtiss-Wright employment dropped from 9,000 to 2,000. The company had meanwhile tried but one fighter design, the XP-31, a strut-braced low-wing monoplane, following its long line of successful biplane fighters of the previous decade; but the XP-31 had been passed over in favour of the Boeing P-26 when the Army ordered 111 P-26s in January, 1933.

It is generally accepted that the US Army's first low-wing all-metal fighter was inspired by the civilian racing planes of that era, beginning with the Travel Air 'Mystery Ship' of 1929, which could fly circles around the military biplane fighters. Indeed, the Thompson Trophy racers of the early 1930s were the

fastest landplanes in the world. True, they mostly consisted of wood, wire, and horse-power, plus some remarkable eye-ball engineering, but the message they offered was not ignored by the US Army Air Corps.

The Air Corps' principal problem was lack of money. No funds were available for the development of high-horsepower aircraft engines; and private industry was understandably moving slowly in that direction because it appeared unlikely that big-engine research and development costs could be recovered from the relatively small orders to be expected from the military.

Still, the Air Corps could dream a little, and push the state of the art to its limits by issuing broad specifications for new fighters that should bring to the surface the best aeronautical engineering talent around. For the 1935 fighter competition their basic specs called for an all-metal, low-wing craft with a speed of 300mph. In view of the fact that Britain and Germany were still buying biplane fighters, and the Air Corps' new P-26 could do but 230mph (its wire-braced wings, fixed landing gear, and open cockpit were vestiges of its biplane heritage), these requirements did represent the absolute maximum that could be hoped for. In fact, not even the most advanced airframe could meet these specs without more power than was then available.

This was well understood by both the Air Corps and engineer Don Berlin. Clearly, 1,000hp was necessary to achieve the 300mph targeted top speed of the new fighter. The best radial engines were then producing up to 750hp, while the only liquid-cooled, high-horsepower engine on the horizon, the Allison V-1710, was still in a state of leisurely development, less than 20 test models having been built. (Development of Britain's legendary Merlin almost exactly paralleled, time-wise, Allison development.)

Nevertheless, Curtiss-Wright President Ralph Damon had given his company an excellent shot at the Air Corps' slightly impossible target when he picked Don Berlin to design the C-W Model 75. Berlin, following graduation from Purdue University in

1921, had spent five years operating the wind tunnel at the Army's McCook Field (later, Wright Field, and now Wright-Patterson AFB); three years with Douglas as chief production design engineer, and five years with Northrop, where he engineered the pioneering all-metal, stressed-skin Alpha, Beta, Gamma aircraft conceived by Jack Northrop. Berlin is a brilliant, methodical man, and admits today that he tended to be a little stubborn when he was younger.

In accepting the job at C-W, Berlin demanded and was promised total control over his assigned project. He knew from experience that every successful aircraft design must have an 'engineering son-of-a-bitch' (as X-15 test pilot Scott Crossfield later termed it in *Always Another Dawn*, by Scott Crossfield and Clay Blair, Jr, World Publishing Co, New York, 1960), someone who has the authority and determination to say 'no' to those who would modify-to-death a promising new design. On several occasions, Berlin was forced to call upon Ralph Damon to rescue Design 75 from in-house tampering by other C-W engineers.

The prototype Hawk 75 made its maiden flight in mid-April 1935 fitted with an experimental Wright R-1670 engine, a twin-row radial of 900hp. The airframe was near-perfect, requiring only a small amount of additional rudder area to improve yaw control at very low airspeeds. The engine was a different matter. It was, in Berlin's words, 'A clunker', and was soon abandoned by Wright enginemen.

Competing aircraft – Seversky, Northrop, and Consolidated – had similar problems, and, after two postponements which ran the competition into April 1936, during which time an experimental Pratt & Whitney R-1535 (also later abandoned) and a new Wright R-1820 Cyclone were tried in the Model 75 Curtiss, de Seversky's aircraft was

declared the winner and the Air Corps purchased 77 of them as Seversky P-35s. The Army ordered three Hawk 75s as service test models, designated them Y1P-36s, and asked that they be powered with the new P&W R-1830 Twin Wasp. Don Berlin recalls: 'The R-1830 engine proved to be the best to date for us and we took one of the Y1P-36s to the fighter competition held at Wright Field in May 1937, and won. The Air Corps ordered 210 of these craft in June 1937 and soon afterwards the French bought 200 of the export version.'

This aeroplane, known as the P-36 to the US Army Air Corps, and called by France's Armée de l'Air the H75 Chasse 1, was eventually sold to 10 other countries as the Curtiss H75 under 15 different dash-numbers or suffixes. Some were delivered with fixed landing gears (H75-H, M, N, O and Q models); most were Cyclone-powered. Those delivered to France and Great Britain were fitted with P&W R-1830-SC3G engines of 1,050hp, or the P&W R-1830-S1C3G of 1,200hp. The British, of course, called their H75s 'Mohawks'.

The P-36/H75 was easy to maintain and a joy to fly. It was highly manoeuvrable, had no bad habits, and its airframe had been

Below: **The prototype Hawk 75 was also fitted with a Wright R-1820 Cyclone of 850hp. Later, many export production models were so powered.**/*Don Berlin*

Bottom: **Designer Donovan R. Berlin's experience with the Northrop Alpha and Beta (pictured), featuring all metal, stress-skin construction, was evident in his Model 75 design at Curtiss-Wright.**/*Don Berlin*

Above: **Wooden mockup of Design 75.**/*Don Berlin*

Right: **Static load test of H75 (P-36) wing, March 1935.**/*Don Berlin*

designed to accept engines of up to twice the power then available. Its fuselage, of semi-monocoque construction, was built in two halves and joined at a horizontal centre-line after installation of internal components. Construction was bulkhead and stringer, with 24St Alclad aluminium alloy skin. The two main wing panels were mated on the vertical centre-line with bridge-plate angles secured by heavy bolts. This saved the weight of a carry-through structure while retaining unusual strength. Wing construction was multi-spar, and the aerofoil was the NACA 2215 at the roots, uniformly tapering to 2209 at the tips. The wing incorporated split flaps, and the balanced ailerons were fabric-covered. Rudder and elevators were also fabric-covered.

Delivery of the first P-36s to the Air Corps began in April 1938; and to put this in perspective timewise, we should note that deliveries of the first Messerschmitt Bf109Bs

Left: The H75 wing, as all Hawk wings to follow, was joined at the centre-line and required no carry-through structure.

Below: The Hawk 75 main landing gear rotated 90 degrees for rearward retraction, and remained unchanged on subsequent Hawks except for shortened oleo struts beginning with the P-40D Model.

and the Hawker Hurricane Mk Is, had begun to the Luftwaffe and RAF, respectively, the previous autumn.

During the time the P-36s were in delivery, the US Air Corps possessed but six pursuit groups, the 1st, 8th, 15th, 16th, 18th and 20th, and all received at least one squadron of the new Hawks (three squadrons of 36 aircraft each, plus reserves, constituted a group). On the eve of the Pearl Harbor attack, this had been expanded to 25 groups, and later in the war would total 74 fighter groups – the pursuit groups having been redesignated 'fighter' groups in May 1942.

Meanwhile, Donovan Berlin had been promoted to chief engineer of the C-W Airplane Division at Buffalo, NY, and working closely with the Air Corps technical people, including Capt Ben Kelsey, Fighter (Pursuit) Project Officer, was looking down the road to future Air Corps' needs. As always, the prime need was for more power, especially, power developed at higher altitudes for greater efficiency.

In 1937, the most promising fighter engines appeared to be the P&W R-1830 and the Allison V-1710. Therefore, Berlin directed, with Air Corps blessing, the mating of a P-36 airframe with an Allison V-1710-11 fitted with a General Electric turbo-super-charger. Designated the XP-37, this craft did achieve its projected 340mph at 20,000ft on those occasions when its turbo unit was operating properly. The Army ordered 13 service test YP-37s in December 1937, hoping that the turbo units could be perfected; but it would be another five years before America possessed a truly combat-ready exhaust-

driven turbo-supercharger, and the YP-37s expired quietly.

Although turbo-supercharger research had been carried on at McCook and Wright Fields since 1918, lack of funds – and metal alloys capable of withstanding the pressures and high operating temperatures – had severely limited progress. The British, on the other hand, had placed their supercharger bets on gear-driven units and, with the priceless experience gained from the Rolls-Royce engines that powered their record-setting Supermarine racers of 1929 and 1931, were clearly ahead of US aircraft engine builders in this soon-to-be critical area.

Had the Allison V-1710 been developed with a gear-driven two-stage, two-speed supercharger similar to that of the Rolls-Royce Merlin 60, much of the 1942-1945 air war history would be different. An ancient aeronautical adage holds that aeroplanes are sometimes worse, but never any better than the engines that power them.

However, at Curtiss, Don Berlin did all that he could with what was available to him at the time. He asked Allison to step-up the rpm of their engine's single-stage blower, and this resulted in 1,090hp at 2,950 engine rpm at 10,000ft. This engine, the V-1710-19, was installed in a P-36 airframe to make the XP-40. The XP-40, following some detailed aerodynamic clean-up, turned in a top speed of 365mph at 15,000ft using carburettor ram-air pressure.

This aircraft, with its radiator located on the aft belly was first flown on 14 October 1938. Three months later, it easily won the 1939 fighter competition at Wright Field, which resulted in an Air Corps order for 524 production P-40s. The production aircraft had the radiator mounted forward under the nose because, Don Berlin says, C-W management thought it looked better that way.

Delivery of the P-40s to the Air Corps began on 1 June 1940.

In the meantime, the never-ending quest for improved performance prompted Curtiss to send a P-36 airframe to Pratt & Whitney where P&W engineers installed an R-1830-31 radial engine that was totally enclosed within a bullet-shaped cowling. A small air scoop beneath the prop spinner provided tunnel cooling. This aircraft was designated the XP-42; but it, too, was abandoned after a number of tests flights determined that its best speed was a disappointing 342mph.

Earlier, in September 1939, work had begun on a smaller fighter at Curtiss. It had Air Corps designation XP-46, and two examples were built to meet an Air Corps' specification that apparently grew from the desire of Gen Henry H. Arnold, Chief of Air Corps, to obtain a ligher, smaller fighter aircraft than those in inventory or under development. Gen Arnold had been impressed by the performance of a French racing plane, the Caudron C-460, flown by Michael Detroyat to decisive victories in both the Greve and Thompson Trophy races at Cleveland in 1936, and had sent Ben Kelsey, his fighter project officer, to inspect the Caudron.

Kelsey, of course, had reported to Arnold that, by the time such a craft was transformed into a useful fighter, it would no longer be as small or as light in weight. However, it seems apparent that Gen Arnold never did completely accept the fact that he couldn't have such a machine if only Wright Field and US planemakers would just try a little harder.

The Curtiss XP-46, which obviously had a great deal of P-40 in it, ended up with an empty weight 100lb heavier than the P-40. It had 10 guns, armour plate, self-sealing fuel tanks, Handley Page wing slats, and a top speed of 410mph fitted with a P-40

engine (V-1710-39). It first flew on 15 February 1941. Just what its performance might have been at altitude with, say, a two-stage Merlin engine, we'll never know.

Or maybe we do know. Here's how Gen (ret) Ben Kelsey relates it:

'Early in 1940, the British Purchasing Commission wanted to buy more P-40s. Well, they had some on order, but the balloon went up and they asked us how many we could build per day.

'Arnold was at Dayton one day, talking to Gen Echols, and Echols told him if we just could hold-off building P-40s for a while, and not try to build it up, we could rush the P-46 through and substitute the P-46 for the P-40 in the build-up, and then we'd have the aircraft we should have, and not the one that was locked into the 1936

procurement, which was . . . an aircraft four years old.

'Echols and Arnold walked down the hall together. Arnold was impressed and said he would check it out in Washington and let us know.

'The next day, or the day after, he called back and said, "We're committed to a training programme with a great many pilots; to a deployment programme that involves the creation and commissioning of new groups, etc . . ."

'Arnold never did tell anyone why he made certain decisions; and this is all the detail he went into. So, the stage was set: every P-40 we could get out of that plant was already obligated. The British wanted as many as they could get . . . My understanding of it is that Echols made a suggestion

Top: **Curtiss Model 75 in original configuration, fitted with the experimental Wright R-1670 engine, a twin-row radial of 900hp.** /*Don Berlin*

Above: **The Model 75 airframe remained basically unchanged throughout Hawk production which ended in November 1944; this photograph was taken 7 August 1935.**/*Don Berlin*

13

to the British, saying if they could find a manufacturer who wasn't already bogged-down in high-priority stuff, that we would make available all the data we had on the P-46 to help them build a new fighter. This was kind of a secret in our talk in the halls about getting P-46s in place of the P-40, to find some way of getting around the problem.

'I don't know how the British got hold of Dutch Kindelberger. I know the way it came back to me was that the British found that North American could do it. Some say that North American bought P-40 data. I don't know what it was for certain; I never saw it. But the rest of the quid pro quo was that three of the very first aircraft would come to us for evaluation.

'Bill Ballhouse, Dutch Kindleberger, and Lee Atwood did an absolutely superb job on the P-51; but the wing area, the placement of the underwing radiator, and the weight – almost everything except the drag, which they cleaned up, and a few other structural details, was like the original P-46. This gave North American a whole start. They didn't have to make a whole bunch of preliminary design studies. They were able to put in their own match angles and their own desires as to where to cut the parts for production; and they were able to determine how much weight went into the armament. They knew what all the equipment specifications were. The 120-day wonder makes sense now. You take a three-view drawing and just refine it to match your own situation.

'Meanwhile, we still wanted the P-46 to replace the P-40. This had nothing to do with the P-51. We were working out our own problems; but there were two things, time and money, that killed the P-46.

'Now, these things don't come out. Everybody who's working on this kind of thing is sure he has all the answers. I don't have all the answers. All I know is the part we had . . . '

Perhaps we should add that one of Mr Kindleberger's oft-repeated axioms was, 'You can't pull a rabbit out of a hat unless you carefully put a rabbit into the hat beforehand'.

Was that a P-46 rabbit you carefully put into the P-51 hat, Mr Kindleberger?

Don Berlin, meanwhile, was ready to make a superior fighter aeroplane of the P-40. He had gone to Britain in May 1941 to question combat-wise RAF pilots about the relative performances of RAF and Luftwaffe fighters. While there, he was mistakenly admitted to a Rolls-Royce test stand where the Merlin 60 was being run. Highly excited, he copied all the test data which he immediately sent back to the US with an embassy courier in a diplomatic pouch. A sizeable flap ensued when it was discovered that someone had goofed and allowed Berlin into the Rolls

secret test area, but there was nothing to be done about it then.

As far as Don Berlin was concerned, he had found the engine that would exploit the P-40's true potential. The Merlin 60, with a two-speed, two-stage geared supercharger would allow the P-40 to take advantage of design characteristics that Berlin had carefully included seven years earlier. Dr. Berlin says:

'I practically designed the Hawk 75 wing in the wind tunnel. I considered the power then available to me, but also the much greater

Top: **Thirteen Y1P-36s were purchased by the Air Corps prior to the P-36A order. This photo is dated 27 February 1937.** /*Don Berlin*

Above: **The Curtiss XP-46A. Was this the rabbit Dutch Kindleberger carefully put into his P-51 hat?** /*USAF*

15

power I expected later. I was especially concerned with the manoeuvrability at high altitudes and at very low airspeeds. In that regard, the aspect ratio, taper ratio, span loading, and wingtip design had to be such that the aircraft would be capable of violent manoeuvres at high altitude without squashing or rolling-out of tight turns resulting from wingtip stall.

'I knew that past fighter designs often gained up to 90% in horsepower and 40% in engine weight as they developed. This, coupled with the need to provide adequate wing to ensure desirable flight characteristics above 25,000ft, markedly influenced my thinking at the time. It was essential that I look ahead; that I design a fighter of sufficient size to accommodate engine installations of much greater power and weight, and to assume eventual perfection of aircraft superchargers.'

However, Berlin's campaign to get the Merlin 60 (actually, in production, the Merlin 61. Called the 266 by Packard, it was the V-1650-3 to the USAAF) was unsuccessful. During the latter half of 1941, just prior to America's entry into World War II, the Packard Motor Company was cranking-up production of the Merlin 28 (V-1650-1), which had a single-stage, two-speed geared supercharger and produced slightly over 1,100hp at 18,000ft. This engine, which was only marginally

better than the V-1710-39 then being installed in the P-40E, was offered to Curtiss and was fitted to the P-40F model that began rolling off the Buffalo assembly lines early in 1942. Berlin says:

'I was never told why we couldn't have the Merlin 60 instead of the 28, although the engine we needed later went into the P-51, there was no plan at that time to employ it. The P-51 at that time was a British project, Allison-powered, and the USAAF displayed little interest in it until much later.

'The P-51 remained a low-altitude fighter, just as the P-40, for the first couple of years of its life because its Allison engine imposed the same limitations on it, that it did on the P-40.

'Then, when somebody whose voice was heard – I've been told that it was Eddie Rickenbacker, who was in England at the time – urged Gen Arnold to try the Merlin 60 in the P-51, it was done, and the results were so spectacular that you know the rest of that story.

'I'm pleased that our side at last was able to exploit this fine engine; but the point is, we could have done so much earlier if Packard had been given the 60 to produce instead of the Twenty-eight.

'Actually, the low-altitude Merlin we used in the P-40F and P-40L models indirectly caused a problem that the "native" engineers at Curtiss-Wright never understood, because they applied the "fix" to the wrong end of the aircraft.

'The XP-40F went to Wright Field during the summer of 1941, in June or July, I think, and we had a couple of production models flying at the factory late that autumn. One

of them was lost as the result of extreme turbulence over the tail and loss of rudder control in a high-velocity dive.

'Now, as director of engineering, I had the right and the duty to advise on all our projects, but the project engineers were not bound by my advice. I knew what the problem was. In re-designing the air scoop for the Merlin's up-draft carburettor (the Allison employed a down-draft carburettor), they made the opening too large and at high speeds hot air was spilling out of the front of the air scoop and setting up turbulence all along the fuselage. All they needed to do was cut-down the radius of the opening of the air scoop. Instead, they insisted on

Top: **One of the H75-A1s purchased by France with delivery beginning in December 1938. The French designated these craft H75 Chasse Is.**/*NASM*

Above: **A P-36C of the 27th PS, 1st PG in washable camouflage paint for the 1939 war games.**/*USAF*

17

lengthening the fuselage in order to get more leverage with the rudder. I regarded that as very crude engineering.

'By this time, near the end of 1941, it seemed to me that I had outlived my usefulness at Curtiss-Wright. I did not have the authority to match my responsibilities. I was frustrated over the engine situation with the P-40; the P-46 obviously wasn't going anywhere, and I lacked confidence in the engineering staff we possessed. Therefore, I resigned and went with General Motors where I did some other interesting things for the remainder of the war; but that's another story.'

We asked Don Berlin if it was possible that the Merlin 60 series engines simply weren't ready for production late in 1941, and he replied that the Spitfire Mk IX, which entered service in mid-1942, was fitted with

the two-speed, two-stage Merlin 70, which was essentially the same engine.

Thus, the P-40 was fated to do its fighting below 20,000ft. There was plenty of it to be done there; and it's easy to find ex-P-40 pilots today who will tell you that this aircraft gave up nothing to the Messerschmitt Bf109s or anything else the enemy possessed, in a shoot-out at the lower altitudes. True, the P-40 was less manoeuvrable than the Japanese Zero-Sen (*everything* was less manoeuvrable than the Zero), but the Flying Tigers established quite early that the P-40, properly flown, could handle even the nimble Zekes.

When Don Berlin left Curtiss-Wright at the end of December 1941, less than 1,000 P-40s had been built. Before the war's end, 13,736 would be produced. Nevertheless, the basic airframe that had been designed as the H75 model during the winter of 1934-

Below: **The XP-37 as it appeared 8 September 1938.** */USAF*

Bottom: **The XP-40 had radiator located on aft belly. Fitted with an Allison V-1710-19 of 1,090hp, this craft first flew 14 October 1938.** */Don Berlin*

1935, was not greatly tampered with through the 30 or so P-40 versions to see combat.

The P-40 through the P-40C, powered with the Allison V-1710-33, was Curtiss model H81, and the Tomahawk Mks I and II to the British and Commonwealth Nations. The H87 model began with the P-40D (Kittyhawk Mk I), which was fitted with the V-1710-39, and appeared with an enlarged radiator air scoop, along with a re-designed canopy and higher propeller thrust-line. This engine, Allison's F3R model, was rated at 1,150hp at 3,000rpm at 12,000ft.

The Merlin-powered P-40F, in production when Berlin resigned, was called the 'Warhawk' by the USAAF (The US Army Air Corps became the US Army Air Forces on 20 June 1941) as were all subsequent P-40s. Also, all subsequent P-40s were H87 models, with suffix letters and dash numbers indicating different engines – through the V-1710-115 – and detail changes to the airframe as well as equipment changes. All H87 models were 'Kittyhawks' to the British and Commonwealth Nations.

A note in the Curtiss-Wright 'Aircraft Billing Ledger' dated 30 November 1944 reads: 'Last production Warhawk, c/n 33956, P-40N-40, s/n 44-47964, delivered this date.'

Of interest, is the modification of a P-40K-1 (s/n 42-45722) which transformed it into the XP-40Q-2. The aft fuselage was cut-down and a bubble canopy fitted; the coolant radiator was considerably slimmed, the wings clipped(!), and – you guessed it – the engine was a Merlin 61 swinging a four-bladed propeller. The actual delivery date of this aircraft to Wright Field is not given, but positioning of the entry in the C-W Aircraft Billing Ledger suggests early 1945. Unfortunately, no performance figures are mentioned.

Other experimental fighters were tried at C-W after Berlin's departure – the XP-55, XP-60, XP-62; the XF14C-2 and XF15C-1 for the Navy, and, finally, the jet-powered XF-87 – but none was successful.

Curtiss-Wright discontinued its Airplane Division in 1950. ('Airplane' is an American word coined in 1916.) It should have been a sad day, but it probably wasn't because the people who had contributed the most to C-W's 40 years' of leadership in this field had long since left the company.

The company's beginnings may be traced back to 1909, when Glenn Hammond Curtiss and Augustus M. Herring formed a corporation to manufacture aeroplanes. Curtiss was an established designer of motorcycle engines, and had built and flown a pusher biplane, the *June Bug*, a year earlier as a partner in the Aerial Experiment Association, a small group funded by Alexander Graham Bell. Herring was a former associate of Octave Chanute in gliding experiments.

The Herring-Curtiss company was dissolved after producing a machine for the Aeronautic Society of New York, and the Curtiss Rheims Racer with which Curtiss won the first Gordon Bennett Trophy race at Rheims, France in 1909.

Curtiss' success was largely due to his engines, small, water-cooled V-8s; and his Curtiss Aeroplane Company prospered with the formation of aerial exhibition teams, aircraft sales, and the training of military aviators at North Island, CA. Through 1916, Curtiss built two-thirds of the 82 aircraft ordered by the US Army and Navy, exported 30 or so to Western Europe and Russia, and fought a series of rearguard court actions with the Wright brothers who charged patent infringement (the Wright's principal patent covered their system of lateral control, wing

Above: **The P-40F, Merlin-powered, had no carburettor air scoop on the cowl. Craft pictured belonged to the 33rd FG in North Africa, and is the stretched fuselage P-40F-5.**/*US Army*

Top: **C-W management asked Berlin to move radiator forward under the nose of production P-40s because it 'looked better' there.**/*USAF*

Above: **The Allison V-1710-33 powered the P-40, P-40B, P-40C, and all Tomahawks.** /*Allison Division, GM*

warping. Curtiss used hinged ailerons, a 1905 French innovation).

By 1916, with the war in Europe two years old and aircraft development accelerating, Curtiss, then 38 years old, felt the need for expansion capital. He allowed financier Clement M. Keys to organise the Curtiss Aeroplane and Motor Corporation, and the resulting stock issue was quickly bought up by automobile interests. Glenn Curtiss remained a top official of this company until his death in 1930.

During World War I, Curtiss was America's largest aircraft builder, its chief product being the JN-4D *Jenny* trainer, powered with the Curtiss OX-5 engine, a water-cooled V-8 of 90hp.

Throughout the 1920s the company was best known for its series of biplane fighters, the Curtiss Hawks, which were fitted with 400hp Curtiss D-12 engines (designed by Charles Kirkham, Curtiss' chief engineman since before World War I), and the 600hp Conqueror, developed from the D-12. These engines were liquid-cooled V-12s, as were the Allisons and Merlins that came later. The Conqueror was deemed to have reached the peak of its development by 1932, at which time the Air Corps began looking hopefully at the new Allison.

In 1929, the Curtiss Aeroplane & Motor Company (the slight name change due to reorganisation in 1923) merged with the Wright Aeronautical Corporation to form Curtiss-Wright Aeronautical Corporation. It seemed a practical union; Curtiss was big in airframe building, and Wright – formed in 1919 from the liquidated remains of the World War I Wright-Martin Company – was a major aircraft engine builder, having developed the famed Whirlwind and Cyclone series of air-cooled radials.

The Curtiss-Wright Aeronautical Corporation seemed destined to play forever a major role in America's developing aircraft industry. It soon controlled 29 subsidiaries, and although the Great Depression of the early 1930s left the giant company gasping for breath for a time, it would, 10 years later, employ 80,000 workers – a high percentage of them building P-40s.

The authors solicited some comments on

Left: **Pursuit Project Officer for the US Army Air Corps during the late 1930s was 1-Lt Benjamin Kelsey.**

Above: **The XP-42 resulted from an attempt by Pratt & Whitney to enclose fully an R-1830-31 engine (with extended prop shaft), but there was no performance gain.**/*Francis H. Dean*

the P-40 from the late William Stubbs, who flew with the US 9th Air Force in the Mediterranean Theatre of Operations (MTO) and here are Bill's replies to our questions (the opinions of others will appear in following chapters):

'The dangling tail-wheel seen in so many P-40 photos was not a rare sight. No cause could firmly be found for this, but the best guess was that after the gear reached the "UP" position and the hydraulic pressure built up to normal, the pilot may have overshot when returning the selector to the neutral position. The landing gear warning horn was not wired through the tail wheel. The hydraulic system was so plumbed that the tail wheel extended first when lowering the gear. Therefore, a very slight amount of hydraulic fluid in the "DOWN line" would have unlocked the tail-wheel up-lock and gravity would do the rest to get the wheel fully extended.

'About Col Robert L. Scott – you'll recall the book he wrote in which he suggests that when he and God fly together, God, being the more inexperienced, rides as co-pilot. This sums up Scott's attitude as described to me by at least one American Volunteer Group (AVG) pilot who knew him well.

'The radio mast on the turtledeck behind the pilot which appeared on some Hawks was for the British VHF radio used on almost all combat planes in the African Campaign. It was built in the US as the SCR522, but this push-button set was of British design and

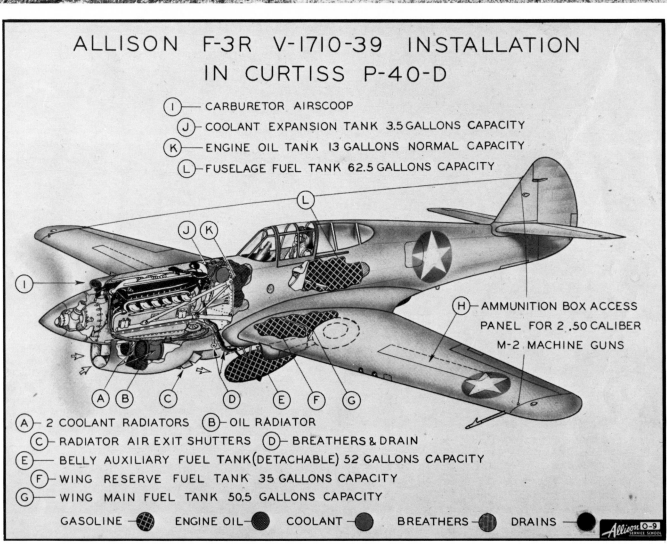

ALLISON F-3R V-1710-39 INSTALLATION
IN CURTISS P-40-D

(I) — CARBURETOR AIRSCOOP
(J) — COOLANT EXPANSION TANK 3.5 GALLONS CAPACITY
(K) — ENGINE OIL TANK 13 GALLONS NORMAL CAPACITY
(L) — FUSELAGE FUEL TANK 62.5 GALLONS CAPACITY

(H) — AMMUNITION BOX ACCESS PANEL FOR 2 .50 CALIBER M-2 MACHINE GUNS

(A) — 2 COOLANT RADIATORS   (B) — OIL RADIATOR
(C) — RADIATOR AIR EXIT SHUTTERS   (D) — BREATHERS & DRAIN
(E) — BELLY AUXILIARY FUEL TANK (DETACHABLE) 52 GALLONS CAPACITY
(F) — WING RESERVE FUEL TANK 35 GALLONS CAPACITY
(G) — WING MAIN FUEL TANK 50.5 GALLONS CAPACITY

GASOLINE —●   ENGINE OIL —●   COOLANT —●   BREATHERS —●   DRAINS —●

Allison 0-9 SERVICE SCHOOL

22

far easier to handle than the USAAF model which required that you turn a dial and "feel" for the proper tone.

'While on the subject of radio installations, there was one annoying thing about the antenna wire that reached from the fin to each wingtip. The lead-in was usually attached on the left side at a point just aft of the direct side-view of the pilot, and this almost-invisible joint had a diverting effect, in that when over water or desert it gave the impression of something moving along the surface. When you turned your head to scan for it, you would find nothing – until you looked straight ahead again and became aware of something from the corner of your eye.

'Yes, the Merlin engine was reliable enough, but it wasn't exactly popular with crews trained on the Allison. The updraft carburettor left it extremely prone to fire in the lower scoop if slightly over-primed in starting. It required a completely different set of wrenches than was needed for airframe maintenance. Also, instead of using glycol for cooling, the Merlin used a mixture of water and glycol which lowered the boiling point to about 160°C, a temperature usually reached in three minutes' of ground operation in the afternoon. The planes had to be towed to the runway for midday take-offs, or else you were suddenly "on instruments" about the time your wheels left the ground as the engine boiled over and sent out a wonderful cloud of steam.

'The true paint colours. Well, the RAF scheme was known as "sand and spinach", the latter due to the shade of green used, and the former due to an item often found in the vegetable – actually, a reddish-brown similar to the colour of dead leaves in the autumn. The lower surfaces were a rather pale blue. For the desert campaign, the "sand" of the original scheme was retained, but the "spinach" was replaced by a dirty yellow, and the description "sand and stone" used. The undersides remained pale blue. All 9th Air Force aircraft in Africa were painted in the RAF "sand and stone" during the desert air war, except for a few B-24s and B-25s which were in "sand" only – and which today is sometimes called "desert pink" by British enthusiasts who fail to recognise the shade of brown as being the same as the RAF "sand and spinach".

'You are right, the P-40 could out-dive just about anything, and indicated airspeeds near 600mph were not unheard of. However, it did want to pull to the right in a dive, and when it was desirable to hold it straight, as for dive-bombing, it needed a lot of left rudder pressure – so much so it was alleged that one could always spot a P-40 pilot by the over-developed muscles in his left leg.'

Left: **The P-40E was six inches shorter than the earlier Hawks; had a slightly narrower fuselage, shorter landing gear legs to eliminate a ground-looping tendency; larger radiator scoop, raised thrust line and six wing guns.** */USAF*

Below: **The Packard-built Rolls-Royce Merlin V-1650-1 (Merlin 28) powered the P-40Fs and P-40Ls.** */Merle C. Olmsted Collection*

Left: **The Allison V-1710-39 was fitted to the P-40D, P-40E, P-40E-1, and the early Kittyhawks.** */Allison Division, GM*

Top: The Kittyhawk Mk I was the same as the P-40D./*USAF*

Top Right: The P-40K-1 and K-5 models had dorsal fins which made them the ugliest Warhawks. Later K models had the long fuselage. RAF fin flash on these K-1s indicates that they served with the 57th or 79th FG early in 1943 while these units fought with the Desert Air Force./*USAF*

Above: The fastest Warhawk at 378mph was the lightweight P-40N-1, which had a reduced fuel capacity, less armour, and four wing guns./*USAF*

Right: The P-40E assembly line at C-W plant No 2, Buffalo, NY; 1942. C-46 Commandos in background./*NASM*

Top: **The Curtiss XP-55 Ascender, fitted with a V-1710 of 1,325hp, was tested during the war but not developed.**/*USAF*

Above: **The 420mph XP-40Q offered too little too late.** /*USAF*

Right: **Glenn Curtiss (left) is pictured in 1911 with Chance Vought (third from right) who also would sell aircraft to the US military.** /*US Navy*

2 The Desperate Days:
Pearl Harbor, Philippines, Aleutians

Despite the hope, held by most Americans, that America could avoid direct participation in World War II, many, perhaps most, felt that sooner or later the US would be drawn into that ever-widening conflict. Whatever the official position of the US Government, the American free press, as always, had provided to the people a handle on reality. So, the people knew.

They didn't know when, and none expected it to come when it did. But having long sensed that the terrible trial was surely inevitable, when it did come, in the form of a surprise attack by the Japanese on the great US Naval and air bases at Pearl Harbor, it did not, as the enemy expected that it would do, leave America frightened and divided. There was no wringing of hands, no cries of doom; only an outraged anger and grim determination to fight. Seldom, in fact, have Americans been so united in a single purpose.

When the Japanese strike force left Pearl Harbor that Sunday morning 7 December 1941, it left behind 2,400 American dead and incredible destruction. But it also left the certainty that Japan and her Axis partners would pay the ultimate price for this monstrous blunder. There would be no negotiated peace. America and her Allies would accept nothing less than unconditional surrender from the Imperial Japanese Government, Nazi Germany, and Fascist Italy.

The attack had come in two waves, beginning at 0755 hours. A total of 352 aircraft participated, flying from six aircraft carriers, 171 Type 99 Val dive bombers, 102 Type 97 Kate attack bombers, and 79 A6M2 Type 0 fighters.

These forces struck simultaneously at the Navy's capital ships anchored around Ford Island, at Hickam Field just south of the harbour where a dozen B-17s and A-20s, along with 17 obsolete B-18s were parked; at the Marine airfield at Ewa and the Navy installation at Kaneohe, and at the Air Corps' fighter base, Wheeler Field, some 12 miles north of Pearl Harbor. Wheeler was home for the 15th and 18th Pursuit Groups, and on the field were 79 P-40Bs and 30 P-36As.

The 44th PS of the 18th PG was at Bellows, about six miles down the coast from Wheeler, with 12 P-40Cs; and the 47th squadron with eight P-40Bs and six P-36As, was at Haleiwa, a dirt strip on the north coast of Oahu, for gunnery qualification.

Lt Harry Brown was a member of the

Left: **A Japanese Navy Zero fighter is launched from Adm Nagumo's strike force early on the morning of 7 December 1941 for the surprise attack on Pearl Harbor and other installations on Oahu.**
/US Navy

Top right: **Living quarters at Bellows Field, Hawaii, 1940.** /*Henry J. Straub*

Centre right: **Curtiss P-36s of the 6th PS, 18th PG, at Wheeler Field, 1940.** /*Henry J. Straub*

Below: **Wheeler Field, 1940.** /*Henry J. Straub*

Bottom: **A P-40C of the 78th PS, 15th PG, Bellows Field, 1941.** /*Henry J. Straub*

47th PS, and one of the handful of American pilots to get into the air to oppose the attackers that morning:

'I did a lot of other things in World War II that I'm prouder of than my actions that day. I later flew with the 475th FG, and what an outfit that was. But you asked about the Pearl Harbor attack.

'Well, the 47th had been sent out to the boonies to live in tents until we qualified in aerial gunnery. I qualified on December sixth, and was released back to civilization. I spent the night in Honolulu celebrating, and was back in my room at the BOQ on Wheeler Field early Sunday morning. Johnny Daines was there and we were having a nightcap together and preparing for bed when we heard an aircraft winding-up overhead.

'This was not too unusual on a Sunday morning. The Navy often got their jollies by pushing everything to the firewall and beating-up our field, correctly assuming that some of us were hung-over. We heard an explosion and thought perhaps that the guy had clobbered himself. So, I went down the hall to take a look, stuck my head out the door, and found the sky literally full of meatballs.

'I shouted to Johnny, but he insisted on delaying the war until he found his socks. He finally did, and we jumped in my car and raced to the flight line at Wheeler. It was pretty much a mess. All the planes had been pushed down to one end of the quadrangle the day before so we could form-up for SMI, and one bomb in the middle of that had pretty much of a domino effect. Also, some genius had arranged for two million rounds of ammunition to be stored in a hangar right in the middle of the flight line and of course the Japanese were concentrating on that and it was all letting go.

'Johnny and I decided to go by and pick up our instructor, Bob Rogers, and then go to Haleiwa where the gunnery planes were. On the way out, a Japanese Kate picked us up and chased us the whole way, first making a pass on us with a full deflection shot, then chandelling so his rear gunner could have a shot. Had he simply lined up on us he couldn't have missed. I didn't realise that we were leading him right to the field at Haleiwa; and when we got there, he had a real field day. After chasing me around a tree a couple of times, he went to work on the parked aircraft and succeeded in setting two of those afire before he buzzed off.

'Kenny Taylor and Jack Welch had arrived just ahead of me, and they latched-onto the two remaining P-40s. I got airborne in a P-36. Standard armament on the P-36 was one .30cal and one .50cal synchronised through the prop. The solonoid was out on the .50cal, so I squeaked into the war with the equivalent of a small calibre deer rifle.

'I climbed up to 10,000ft and went over to Bellows Field. I could hear a lot of chatter on the air. I started to Wheeler and saw another plane, low-wing, looked like a Japanese fighter. I had the altitude and dived to the attack and almost shot down Bob Rogers in another P-36. I pulled in close to his wing and he pointed downward to an enemy Kate. Rogers motioned to me to peel-off and take him, but I indicated that I would follow since I was a bit short of firepower.

'Rogers went down after the Kate and fired a short burst from about 400yd and I followed. We went round and round, and finally the Kate went straight down with me after him. Then, he chopped his throttle and dumped his dive brakes and I went shooting past him. At this point, I suddenly realised that I could recognise individual white caps on the water below. I barely missed the water, I think, and went up onto my back into a big fat cumulus cloud while blacked-out from the sharp pull-up. You want to know who really invented the lomcevak? Try stalling-out a P-36 on its back inside a cloud sometime, while trying all sorts of desperate things with the controls!

'I've often wondered if the Japanese pilot made it home. I didn't get him, and Rogers didn't get him, but there's a good chance that he spun-in while laughing uncontrollably at our antics.

'I heard Rogers shouting something, and I looked out over Barber's Point and saw two enemy aircraft. Rogers took one and I chose one and sort of stuck my prop up his tail and pulled the trigger. When he began to burn, I Immelmanned-out and found myself face-to-face with a flight of 10 or 15 Japanese planes. I barrelled through them and they were so surprised that none fired a shot.

'I turned back to see if I could do some mischief and saw another P-36 trying to sneak up on them. I thought it was Rogers, but it turned out to be a guy named Mike Moore. He and I formed up and gave chase. I let him lead. He chose a straggler and we chased that one all over the sky. I followed him out to sea after Mike ran out of ammunition. I fired the last ammo I had, and he was trailing smoke as I broke off. I later learned that he crashed ashore, and I was given credit for the victory; but it could have just as well been Mike who hit him.

'I have often claimed that I'm the only man in the US Air Force to have scored two kills while wearing a tuxedo; but actually I flew that day dressed in tux trousers, pyjama tops, and house shoes.

'I think it is interesting to note that the first American aerial victory of the war was probably scored in a P-36. Johnny Daines was flying one, as was Rogers, Gordon Sterling, Tony Thacker and I. The only P-40s I know of that got into the air were flown by Welch and Taylor.'

It isn't possible to say, with certainty, who got the first air victory that morning. Lt George Welch, flying a P-40, shot down four of the attackers. Kenneth Taylor damaged one before he himself was wounded. Johnny Daines was shot down by US Army anti-aircraft gunners near Hickam Field.

Meanwhile, the 44th PS, at Bellows, got three of its P-40s fuelled and armed about an hour after the attack began. Lts George Whitman, Hans Christianson and Sam Bishop were taking-off in these craft when six Zeros approached for a strafing run. Christianson's P-40 was exploded during his take-off run.

Whitman was shot down immediately after lift-off, and Bishop had his controls shot out at about 400ft. He went into the ocean, but swam ashore unhurt. The Zeros then destroyed seven of the remaining nine P-40s at Bellows where they sat.

The attack ended at approximately 0945 hours, when the last enemy aircraft left the area to return to their carriers. In addition to the 2,400 American dead, 1,500 were wounded. The battleships *Arizona, Oklahoma, West Virginia* and *California* were sunk, and 14 other ships heavily damaged. The Navy and Air Force lost 233 aircraft, plus 159 damaged. A total of 27 P-40s and 16 P-36s remained flyable. According to Japanese records, the enemy lost 28 aircraft in the attack.

During the next few hours, the Japanese also struck at British Malaya, Thailand, Singapore, Hong Kong, Guam, Midway, Wake Island and the Philippines.

Word of the surprise attack on Pearl Harbor was flashed to the world by Navy radio 34 minutes after the first bombs fell, or at 0829 hours Honolulu time. It was then 0259 hours, 8 December, in the Philippines where Adm Hart's radioman picked up the stunning message. Adm Hart immediately alerted the headquarters of Gen Douglas MacArthur, and British, Dutch, and Chinese forces in his area.

The Japanese strike in the Philippines would not come until 1130 hours – almost nine hours after word of the attack on Pearl Harbour had been received there. Still, when it did come it met no organised resistance. Air Force's Gen Lewis Brereton, who had assumed command of the newly created Far East Air Force (FEAF) only the day

before, was at Gen MacArthur's Manila headquarters by 0500 hours seeking permission to send his 17 B-17s (he had an additional 15 B-17s at Del Monte Airfield on Mindanao, 500 miles to the south) against Japanese airfields on Formosa, from where an enemy air attack on the Philippines must – and did – come. But Gen MacArthur was 'too busy' to see his air commander, and MacArthur's chief of staff, Gen Southerland, told Brereton that Americans should not fire the first shot in that part of the world.

The FEAF officially contained 162 fighter aircraft, including the 6th Philippine Pursuit Squadron's 11 obsolete Boeing P-26As. The USAAF 24th PG – consisting of the 17th, 20th, 21st, 34th and 3rd Pursuit Squadrons – possessed 72 P-40s and 35 Seversky P-35s in commission, plus 35 P-40s and 11 P-35s in maintenance or grounded for lack of parts. The group commander was Maj Orin C. Grover. Other aircraft included 34 B-17s, of the 19th Bomb Group, plus some 25 miscellaneous craft such as O-47s, O-52s, and a handful of old B-18s. The observation planes, and 17 of the B-17s, were stationed at Clark Field, near Manila. The remaining B-17s were at Del Monte, 500 miles to the south on the big island of Mindanao.

The 3rd PS, at Iba Field, commanded by Lt Henry J. Thorne, had 15 P-40s and six P-35s. The 34th PS at Del Carmen, led by Lt S. H. 'Sam' Merritt, had 29 P-35s. Lt Boyd 'Buzz' Wagner was CO of the 17th PS at Nichols Field with 18 P-40s. The 21st PS also at Nichols, possessed 16 P-40s in commission, and was commanded by Lt Edward Dyess. The 20th PS was temporarily stationed at Clark Field with 23 flyable P-40s and Lt Joseph H. Moore in command.

Lt-Gen (ret) Joseph Moore recalls some of the events of those critical hours:

'We were told of the attack on Pearl Harbor at about 0430 hours and spent most of the morning awaiting orders. During the last hour and a half before the attack came, we were in our cockpits ready to take-off on very short notice.

'Our warning system depended upon a network of ground observers and telephones which were on the primitive side. There was an early model radar unit – highly secret – at Iba, but as things turned out it was as useless as our telephones when most needed. When the attack came, which we were fully expecting, there was no warning at all. We later learned that there was some sabotage, and what was then called "fifth columnists" (Filipino traitors or enemy agents) at work to render ineffective what little we had in the way of communications.

'Finally, I got tired waiting in my aircraft and got on a bicycle to pedal down to operations to see if they knew anything. They didn't. Then, suddenly, a crew chief called out, "My God, here they come!" And over in the west we saw a long line of aeroplanes, very high, flying line-abreast.

'I got back to my aeroplane, jumped in, kicked rudder, and went off down the field with six of my squadron close behind. I thought the incoming enemy must be from a carrier, so I continued eastward for a little longer than normal so that we could intercept them on the way out, it being already too late, of course, to stop them from coming in.

'When I changed heading to the north, climbing my P-40 at its maximum rate, I looked back and saw the whole field covered with intense black smoke. I had two birds with me. The four following pilots had been killed on the runway, two just airborne and two still rolling. The remaining P-40s were bunched up, taxiing out of their revetments for take-off, and were hit before they got on the runway. Some of those pilots were injured, but none were killed.

'I levelled off at 22,000ft with my number two man, Randy Keator, just behind me. Eddie Gilmore was 2-3,000ft below, trying to catch up. As I turned my attention to the sky ahead again, I saw a flight of nine aircraft coming our way. I first thought it was Hank Thorne from Iba, and waggled my wings; but then I recognised them as Zeros.

'The enemy had spotted Gilmore, but apparently didn't see Keator and me. As they peeled off to attack Gilmore, Keator and I rolled right in behind them, from above and behind, and that's the first and last time I ever got such an advantage over a Zero.

'We got some good hits on several of them, and were later told there were five burning wrecks found on the ground, but we had no time to admire the results of our attack, because I very quickly had three Zeros on my tail, with no time to think about anything else. I tried just about everything, but couldn't shake them until, at last, I split-essed, headed for the deck, and discovered that I could out-dive them.

'On the way back to the field, a single Zero dropped onto my tail from among the cumulus clouds and I barrel-rolled, causing him to speed past me, and gave him a burst from my guns – those that were still firing, that is. I never flew a mission in the Philippines without experiencing gun failure. My squadron had P-40s, which were equipped with two .50s firing over the nose and two .30cals in each wing. We had received these aircraft in mid-1941, but were never allowed to fire our guns – except once, when I was given 50 rounds of ammunition – until war came.

'I circled the field twice while trying to find a place to land that wasn't full of bomb craters. The runway was unusable. They had damaged us greatly. I had 23 P-40s to begin that day; I got three airborne. Of the 20 on the ground, we salvaged two, so the 20th Pursuit Squadron had five serviceable P-40s remaining.'

The 3rd PS at Iba Field fared even worse. Iba was hit about 20 minutes after the strike at Clark Field. Nine P-40Es were on the ground there, and six were in the pattern, returning from a fruitless patrol with near-empty fuel tanks. The incoming Zeros shot down five of the six and destroyed eight of those on the ground. Lt I. B. 'Jack' Donalson accounted for two of the enemy fighters before his engine quit from fuel starvation. He landed safely, however, and the 3rd's two remaining P-40s joined what was left of

Capt Joe Moore's 20th PS, which moved to Lubao and Nielson, a couple of small dirt strips north of Manila.

The 19th Bomb Group lost 16 of its B-17s on the ground at Clark Field in the midday attack.

A few days later, Gen Brereton ordered the 17th PS to join the 20th, and this gave the combined 20th/17th/3rd PSs an average total of 18-20 flyable P-40s, with several in maintenance. 'In maintenance', of course, meant that the fighters were being patched with whatever was available, from bridge timbers to tinned meat cans. Engine oil was strained through makeshift filters and re-used; tail-wheel tyres were stuffed with rags. There was little to be done about the guns. Much of the ammunition was faulty, and the gun lubricants on hand congealed into a gummy mass at altitude. The steadily dwindling number of P-40s and P-35s was owed more to lack of parts and the dusty, near-impossible airstrips than to enemy action.

Below: **Two years after the attack on Pearl Harbor, P-40s remained on alert there, but this P-40K-1 would never see combat.** */USAF*

Too much of the attrition was due to the necessity of cannibalising some aircraft in order to keep others flying.

This betrayal of America's defenders was part of the greater betrayal of all Americans (so eloquently pleaded more than 15 years earlier by Gen Billy Mitchell) resulting from the self-serving ambitions, ignorance and incompetence of four US presidents, the US congresses of the 1920s and 1930s, and top US military leaders dominated by cliques of saddle-horse generals and battleship admirals. Few Americans, however, were to feel that betrayal more keenly than the 15,000 US soldiers, sailors and airmen in the Philippines. These men and women (Army nurses), poorly prepared for war in the first place, were abandoned after war began. That they managed to resist for months, unsupplied and unsupported by their own government, constitutes a saga of courage that clearly deserves a page in history alongside that made by their British cousins, whose unimagined resolve had earlier borne the hell of Dunkirk, and defeated the enemy in spirit long before he was defeated in fact.

This situation occasioned some bitter humour. After being backed-up on the Bataan Peninsula, the Americans referred to themselves as the 'Battling Bastards of Bataan' (no momma, no papa, no Uncle Sam); and a nameless crew chief caused a signal to be sent by Navy radio which read: 'Dear President Roosevelt, please send us another P-40. The one we have is full of holes.'

On 9 December, Nichols and Del Carmen Fields were bombed. The Navy base at Cavite was destroyed on the 10th, and Japanese fighters of the enemy's Fifth Air Group, Army Type 97 (Ki-27) Nates, occupied Vigan Field on Luzon's north coast as the Nipponese came ashore to begin their march on Manila.

By 15 December, the 21st and 34th PSs were at Pilar with about 10 serviceable P-40s and a like number of P-35s, while the 20th and 17th squadrons, at Lubao and Nielson, could count no more than 14 more or less flyable P-40s. During this period, lacking any kind of warning system, the P-40s flew regular patrols, usually with two to four aircraft, sometimes with as many as six; but since the enemy seldom sent less than 30 fighters to accompany his Betty (G4M1-3) and Nell (G3M1-3, Type 96) bombers, the aerial confrontations were decidedly one-sided.

Meanwhile, Lt Buzz Wagner became America's first USAAF World War II ace when he shot down two Nates on the 12th, and followed with four more the next day.

The main Japanese invasion force landed at Lingayen Gulf on 21 December; and on Christmas Eve, Gen Brereton was ordered to Australia, along with the 12 remaining B-17s at Mindanao, while US and Filipino troops, including whatever was left of the FEAF, were evacuated to the Bataan Peninsula, a finger of land encircling Manila Bay on the west. What the FEAF actually had left was 20 P-40s, two P-35s and a PT-13 Stearman biplane.

Any attempt to list the pilot's names who flew from Bataan must inevitably be incomplete because the official records that survived (now at the Air University, Maxwell AFB) are far from complete. We find in these smudged reports the names of Capt Ed Dyess, acting CO, Capts Rowe, Joe Moore, Lunde, Thorne and Barnick, along with

Below: **Lt Boyd D. 'Buzz' Wagner, flying a P-40E, became America's first World War II ace when he shot down six Nates on 12 and 13 December 1941, in the Philippines.**
/*Wide World Photos*

34

Lts Ben Brown, David Obert, Posten, Gehrig, Glover, Stone, Stinson, White, Grashio, Woolery, Ibold, Hall, Baker, Benson, and Capts Randolph, Caldwell, Bradford, Whitfield, and Fellows. Lts Ed Burns and Charles Sprague are mentioned in reports signed by Capt Dyess. There were others, and some, including Buzz Wagner, along with some ground support personnel, who were evacuated safely to Australia after their planes were gone. Some took up rifles and manned ground positions with the infantry.

Manila, declared an 'Open City', was occupied by the advancing Japanese 14th Army on 2 January 1942, and the 15,000 Americans and 45,000 sketchily-trained Filipinos were backed-up on Bataan with little hope for relief, their sole mission to simply hold-out as long as possible.

By mid-January, with but nine P-40s still flyable, Gen MacArthur ordered that combat with enemy aircraft be avoided and the planes saved for reconnaissance only. Militarily, that may have been a proper decision; but it failed to take into account the mood of the pilots, whose every instinct demanded that the enemy pay as dearly as possible for his aggression. Therefore, jury-rigged bomb-release mechanisms were devised to carry 500lb bombs (left behind by the B-17s), and recce missions often included attack on enemy positions as a matter of 'self-defence'.

On 29 January, Lts Woolery and Obert each led a flight of three P-40s to bomb and strafe Nielson and Nichols Fields by moonlight. Fourteen enemy aircraft were destroyed on those captured airfields, along with a number of trucks.

On 9 February, the last six P-40s tangled with a like number of enemy fighters and shot down all of the enemy for the loss of one P-40. The P-40s were accompanying the PT-13, flown by Filipino Air Force Capt Jesus Villamor, on a recce mission to locate enemy artillery that was lobbing fire onto Bataan from nearby mountains. The downed P-40 was flown by Lt Stone, who had four official air victories when he died.

Then on 2 March, Capt Ed Dyess led three of the remaining five P-40s in an attack on enemy shipping in Subic Bay on the southwest coast of Luzon. Dyess got an enemy tanker with his 500-pounder, while Posten, White and Grashio sank a 100 ton motor launch and strafed a supply depot at Olongapo. However, Lt White was lost over the target, while Posten and Grashio's P-40s, badly shot-up, were crash-landed upon their return to the field at Mariveles, Bataan.

Later that same day, Dyess and Lt Burns returned to Subic Bay in the remaining two P-40s to sink an enemy transport ship, but it cost them another aircraft when Burns washed-out his craft upon landing.

For a few days there was but one P-40. Then, the handful of malnourished, dysentery-ridden mechanics who were left managed to piece together another from several wrecks.

Meanwhile, the 'Bamboo Fleet' appeared. It was born of a great need and nurtured almost totally with courage. Capt Joe Moore had flown a P-40 400 miles south to the Island of Cebu to obtain medical supplies. There he found an open-cockpit Waco biplane, and a three-place Bellanca Cruisair which had been commandeered from their prewar civilian owners. These craft, along with a Staggerwing Beech cabin biplane, and a J2F Grumman Duck amphibian resurrected from the water off Mariveles, were pressed into service shuttling between Cebu and Bataan, carrying medical supplies north and evacuating a few USAAF personnel to the south.

Joe Moore was a regular pilot of the Bamboo Fleet, usually at the controls of the two-place Duck:
'It was a bit tough because we never knew what the weather would be, and enemy aircraft were always a threat. We tried to get into or out of Bataan in darkness – late evening or early morning, depending upon which way we were going – so most of the flight would be in daylight. This worked pretty well, but we eventually lost all except the Duck, either to enemy action or to take-off and landing accidents.

'The Stearman PT-13, carrying two pilots in the rear cockpit and another flying the plane from the front, went down on a beach in southern Luzon after those fellows got lost in bad weather. They were rescued. The Beechcraft was shot down by Japanese fighters. The Bellanca crashed in the water several hundred yards offshore at Mariveles. The pilot was asking too much of her and it was dark. The Waco, with three aboard, was shot down between Cebu and Del Monte by two Japanese Navy patrol planes.'

Until early April 1942 the Battling Bastards of Bataan somehow held back the six divisions of the Japanese 14th Army; but then the Invader breached their lines, and on 8 April Gen Jonathan Wainwright, left in command after MacArthur's escape to Australia a month earlier, retreated to the caves of Corregidor Island in Manila Bay with most of the American troops, and sadly ordered the remaining defenders of Bataan to surrender.

Later that day, Lt Donalson struck at enemy positions with a load of fragmentation bombs, then continued southward to Cebu. Capts Lunde and Thorne managed to get off in the two remaining P-35s, each with a pilot in his baggage compartment; and Capt Joe Moore followed in the last Bataan P-40.

All later made it safely to Del Monte in Mindanao.

The last to leave Bataan was Capt Roland Barnick in the Duck. He took-off under heavy fire half an hour after midnight, so overloaded that he needed 150 miles to gain 200ft of altitude. He had five passengers stuffed into the two-place amphibian, one of them famed Filipino soldier/statesman Carlos Romulo. Bataan was surrendered a few minutes later.

Two months before Bataan fell, pilots of the 24th PG evacuated to Australia were re-formed into the 3rd, 17th and 20th Provisional Pursuit Squadrons and re-equipped with P-40Es at Amberly Field, Brisbane. Possessing less than 50 aircraft between them, these squadrons were under strength, and their mission was approximately as impossible as the one from which they had just escaped in the Philippines. They were ordered to Java to reinforce the relative handful of British and Dutch airmen there.

Early in February 1942 the 17th Squadron reached Java with 12 P-40s; the 20th arrived with 10 aeroplanes, eight having been lost in combat en route, while half of the 3rd's 18 P-40s were charged off to weather accidents before reaching their destination. These 31 fighters flew but 150 hours of combat in Java, but accounted for 50 enemy aircraft shot down, plus 15 probables, before the Japanese landed in Java on 1 March 1942, and these pilots were again evacuated back to Australia. Nine of them were killed over Java, and four were missing.

Meanwhile, other USAAF units equipped with P-40s and serving in other sensitive areas included the 16th PG in Panama, the 35th PS of the 36th PG at Ponce Field, Puerto Rico; and the 33rd PS of the 8th PG which went to Iceland in August 1941 with 4,000 US Marines. The 33rd had flown their 30 P-40s the final 100 miles into Reykjavik from the deck of the aircraft carrier *Wasp*.

In Alaska, at the time of the attack on Pearl Harbor, the 28th Composite Group contained 12 B-18s and 20 P-36As spread between newly completed fields at Fairbanks, Nome, Anchorage, Kodiak and Yakutat. Not until 23 May 1942 did the first P-40s arrive at Otter Point and Cold Bay on Umnak Island to protect the Navy base at Dutch Harbour.

Below: **Curtiss P-40C of the 33rd FS, 8th FG, which went to Iceland in August 1941 to preempt possible German seizure of this strategically located island.**/*USAF*

The P-40s belonged to the new 343rd Fighter Group of the new 11th Air Force, and they arrived in the Aleutians none too soon. The Japanese plan to finish off the US Navy in a showdown battle at Midway on 4 June included diversionary strikes at Dutch Harbour the day before, and the landing of Japanese troops on the islands of Kiska and Attu at the outermost tip of the Aleutians on the 6th and 7th.

Lacking radar or any kind of warning system, the fighter pilots in the Aleutians at this time simply flew patrols, weather permitting. Thus it was more by chance than by design that contact with the enemy was made during the initial attack on Dutch Harbor. Lts John B. Murphy and Jacob W. Dixon stumbled upon a pair of enemy Rufes and promptly shot them down. The Rufe, Nakajima A6M2-N, Type 2, was a single-float fighter built around the Mitsubishi A6M2 Zero airframe, and widely employed in the Pacific.

The next day, eight P-40s of the 343rd's 11th FS caught 11 Japanese Kates and 10 carrier-based Zeros over Dutch Harbor and accounted for two Kates and two Zeros before the enemy disappeared into the fog. Lts Chancellor, Dale, White, and Cape were credited with the air victories.

Four P-40s and two pilots, including Lt Cape, were lost to these two encounters, although two of the crippled P-40s were washed out more as a result of deteriorating weather rather than to enemy action. It was later learned that several of the attackers also went down after failing to find their carrier in the fog-shrouded Aleutian waters.

Serving with the 343rd FG until September 1942 were the Kittyhawk-equipped RCAF Nos 14 and 111 Squadrons; but enemy air strength in the Aleutians was never significant – two or three squadrons of Rufes, along with some large flying boats – and the Aleutian weather, along with the enemy's lack of aggressiveness, severely limited the chances for aerial combat.

The three squadrons (11th, 18th, and 54th) of the 343rd FG, fitted with P-38s and P-39s as well as P-40s, mostly bombed and strafed the enemy as new strips were built closer to his bases. Then, after the US 7th Infantry Division wiped out the 1,200-man Nipponese force on Attu in May 1943, the 1,800 Japanese on Kiska boarded ships and slipped away in the Aleutian mists. The 343rd remained on guard in that most hostile of flying environments to fight the weather – which had been their most dangerous enemy from the beginning.

Left: The 33rd's P-40Cs were hoisted to the deck of the Fleet Carrier *Wasp* at Norfolk, Virginia, and then flown the final 100 miles into Reykjavik, Iceland./*US Navy*

Below: In the Aleutians, the principal enemy was the weather: snow, fog, rain and incredible winds./*USAF*

Bottom: This 343rd FG P-40E on Attu in the Aleutians is interesting because its bottom wing surface contains the legend 'US ARMY', a marking discontinued prior to introduction of the H87 series Hawks.

Right: Alexai Point, Aleutians, 27 September 1943; normal weather conditions prevailing. At 200ft, like flying inside a bottle of milk./*USAF*

Below right: The runway at Amchitca in the Aleutians provided an extra thrill on each take-off and landing./*USAF*

3 The Desperate Days:
Battle of France, Early Desert War

While the P-36 and P-40 saw action in American hands almost from the instant the US was plunged into World War II, both aircraft actually had been fighting in the hands of America's allies much earlier.

In June 1938 France ordered 100 Hawk 75s, the export version of the P-36A, which the Armée de l'Air called H75 Chasse Is. Subsequent orders increased the total to 730 machines, although only 619 were built and no more than 225 actually reached France before France surrendered to Germany in June 1940.

However, the 200 or so Hawk 75s that saw combat from the war's beginning in September 1939, until France fell 10 months later, were far and away France's most effective aerial defenders. During the final six weeks of French resistance, the five Hawk-equipped squadrons accounted for one-third of all French air victories, and in the hands of the French fighter pilots, the Hawk 75 appears to have been superior to the Bf109E it met in battle. The French pilots reported that they could turn inside the Messerschmitts, out-climb them, and were at least equal in top speed.

In China, three squadrons (approximately 80 machines) of Hawk 75Ms, the fixed-gear version of the P-36, Cyclone-powered, opposed the invading Japanese as early as May 1938 in China's fledgling air force, while similar aircraft went to Thailand (then Siam) and the Netherlands East Indies in 1938 and 1940 respectively. Both the Thai and Dutch Hawks saw action following the Japanese attacks in December 1941.

Meanwhile, the Russians began receiving P-40s as early as August 1940, and would eventually get 2,091 such craft of various models; but official Soviet Air Force records are not available in the west to document the role played by P-40s in the defence of that country.

Britain received 241 H75 Mohawks, beginning in mid-1940. These were aircraft ordered by France but not delivered. Some were used for training; others went to India, East Africa and Portugal.

Beginning in September 1940, Great Britain took delivery of 1,081 Tomahawks (Models H81-A, -A2, and -A3) and, following up till 1 January 1944, received 3,112 Kittyhawks (H87-A3 to H87-W models). From among these Tomahawks and Kittyhawks, Australia got 943 machines, Canada approximately 360, New Zealand 293 and South Africa 400. Some of these early Tomahawks were later transferred to Russia, Turkey and the Egyptian Air Force. However, most British and Commonwealth Tomahawks and Kittyhawks saw combat.

We may note in passing that the British purchased outright 252 Tomahawks before the US Congress approved the Lend-Lease Bill in April 1941.

When the war began, 3 September 1939, France had some 400 Morane-Saulnier MS405 and 406 fighters, plus 152 Hawk 75s. The Hawk units were the Groupes de Chasse I/4, I/5, II/4, and II/5 (a *groupe* contained 18-24 aircraft consisting of two *escadrilles* of 9-12 planes each). According to C-W representative Jerry Clark, who arrived in France on Christmas Eve 1938 to oversee assembly of the H75s and give each a two-hour test flight, the Hawks out-performed the Morane-Saulniers in all flight regimes, and the pilots assigned to the Hawk groups were France's best.

This was reflected in the combat records to follow. Although the French Air Force saw little action during the six months of the 'Phoney War' period (23 November 1939 to 10 May 1940) while the Germans carefully prepared for the conquest of France, the French Hawk groups accounted for one-third of all French Air Force air victories, or a total of 311 in exchange for 29 Hawk pilots killed from war's beginning until France fell in June 1940. This ranked them 1st, 2nd and 3rd among all the fighter groups in the French Air Force. A fifth Hawk group, III/2, organised just 18 days before French capitulation, was officially credited with 17 victories for the loss of two pilots during the 11 days it was in combat.

In light of the fact that confirmation for aerial victories under French policy was not easily obtained, this record, made against

Above: **A trio of Fairey Battles escorted by a pair of French Hawk 75s over France prior to the fall of France.**/*IWM via Chris Shores*

Left: **French Hawk 75s of Groupe de Chasse I/5 on patrol during the spring of 1940. I/5 Groupe destroyed 111 enemy aircraft while losing nine pilots.**/*INS*

groups were noteworthy, they nevertheless represented relative pin-pricks to the Nazi war machine. During the second week of May 1940, German panzers rolled through Belgium, Holland, and the Ardennes Forest, skirting France's 'impregnable' Maginot Line to encircle and split the British and French armies. Although France was not formally surrendered until 25 June, the Battle of France had been decided by 15 May, only five days after the German offensive began.

Actually, the Battle of France had been decided much earlier. France never recovered from her losses in World War I, and implicit in the defensive thinking of the French High Command was a nationwide hatred of war. Add to that the unstable politics and indecisive leadership of the 1920s and 1930s, plus an unmistakable if latent defeatism simmering just below the surface of France's national conscience, and it becomes clear that France's defeat in 1940 had been in the making since the signing of the Versailles Treaty in 1919.

In Britain and America there were no such national attitudes; but there was – and had been since 1919 – plenty of fuzzy-headed thinking in high places as one government after another appeared to believe that an earnest desire for peace was all that was necessary to insure it. These great nations would also pay dearly for their 20 years of euphoria.

Two weeks before France fell, Italy's fascist dictator, Benito Mussolini, decided that he could earn Hitler's respect, and perhaps expand Italy's African empire, by declaring war on Britain and France. This must have seemed a safe enough proposition to Mussolini immediately following the British evacuation at Dunkirk and with the Germans at the gates of Paris. The Italian colonies in Africa then consisted of Ethiopia, Eritrea, Italian Somaliland and Libya. If Egypt and the Suez Canal could be added, Britain's supply of Middle East oil would be cut off, while any future threat to Italy and Southern Europe from North Africa should be erased, since the rest of North Africa to the west was French controlled.

The Italians in North Africa, however, were poorly motivated and badly led. Their first (and only) major offensive into Egypt, in September 1940, ended with the destruction of the Italian 13th Army, and the British 300 miles into Libya. That forced Hitler to go to Mussolini's aid in North Africa, and the first Luftwaffe aircraft appeared over the western desert on 9 January 1941.

On 1 April Generalleutnant Erwin Rommel led his Deutches Afrika Korps against the victorious British and pushed them back into Egypt. This marked the beginning of a see-saw war in that harsh land that would last for

substantial odds, gives us our best view of the H75 (Mohawk) in combat against a well-equipped and well-trained enemy.

Ironically, the odds against the French military, including the French Air Force, were largely self-imposed by France's leaders. Luftwaffe records reveal that no more than 1,200 Messerschmitt Bf109s and 110s were arrayed against approximately 600 operational fighters (counting RAF Hurricanes based in France) possessed by France's defenders. While odds of two-to-one make for a less than desirable situation, it isn't necessarily an impossible one if the out-numbered defender is well directed, and sufficiently motivated, a fact clearly established by the Battle of Britain. The fragmented direction of the French Air Force was summed up by French troops who adopted a quick means of aircraft identification: 'When there are three planes, they're French. When there are forty, they're Germans'.

If the performances of the French Hawk

more than two years. It was also at that time – mid-April 1941 – that the first Tomahawks arrived in Egypt to play a significant role in the desert war.

These machines were Tomahawk IIBs (H81-A2 and A3s). Some were flown across the Sahara from Tokaradi, on Africa's Gold Coast, and some went by ship around the tip of Africa, through the Gulf of Aden up the Red Sea to Port Sudan. Approximately 40% of those ferried across the Sahara were lost en route, according to C-W representative Jerry Clark, who flew one of those craft himself.

The first Tomahawks equipped Royal Australian Air Force No 3 Squadron, which was held in Syria throughout most of the spring and summer as first Crete, then Greece fell to the Germans. Then, RAAF No 3 Squadron moved to Egypt in late August as it became clear that neighbouring Turkey would remain neutral for the foreseeable future.

In the meantime, other squadrons had been Tomahawk-equipped. RAF No 250 (Sudan) Squadron received its Hawks early in June and claimed the first Tomahawk aerial victory on 8 June, when Flg Off Hamlyn shot down an Italian Cant Z1007 bomber over Egypt. South African Air Force No 2 Squadron was re-equipped with Tomahawks in July; and on 11 August RAF No 112 Squadron came to the desert war from Palestine with new Tomahawks. SAAF No 4 Squadron traded its worn-out Hurricanes for Tomahawks in October.

Thus, when Gen Sir Claude Auchinleck's newly named British 8th Army launched Operation Crusader against the Germans and Italians on 18 November 1941, there were five Tomahawk squadrons (and seven Hurricane squadrons) in Air Chief Marshal Arthur Tedder's Desert Air Force. In opposition were some 250 Luftwaffe aircraft and 170 machines of the Regia Aeronautica. Among these were four staffeln of Bf109Fs and one

43

staffel of Bf109Es belonging to JG27,* three staffeln of Bf110Ds of I/ZG26, a staffel of Ju88A-4s of I/LG1, and six squadriglie of Macchi Mc202s. Later, JG53 and JG77 (Bf109Fs and Gs) would be sent to aid Rommel.

Operation Crusader sent Rommel reeling back over his own tracks all the way to El Agheila, halfway across Libya, which was where he had started from the previous April. The retreating Germans and Italians were hounded all the way by the Desert Air Force.

The Hawks and Hurricanes were largely in control of the air over Libya during Crusader because the enemy was obsessed with the need to destroy British naval and air bases on the Island of Malta, located between Sicily and Tunisia where the Mediterranean is but 200 miles across. Malta not only protected British shipping from Gibralter to Alexandria, as well as the Suez Canal at its most dangerous point, it also threatened the Axis supply route from Italy and Sicily to North Africa. Much of the air power that would otherwise have been available to Rommel from Sicily, including four gruppen of Bf109Fs of JG53, was pre-occu-

*In the Luftwaffe, a *Staffel* contained 9-12 fighters, and three *Staffeln* made a *Gruppe*, the basic fighter unit. Three *Gruppen* made a *Geschwader*, and each *Geschwader* was identified according to mission. Thus, *Jagdgeschwader* (JG), single-engine fighters; *Kampfgeschwader* (KG), bombers; *Stukageschwader* (StG), dive bombers, and *Zerstorergeschwader* (ZG), Bf110 Destroyers. There were two so-called 'elite' wings designated 'LG' for *Lehrgeschwader*.

Regia Aeronautica *squadriglie* consisted of nine aircraft each, and three *squadriglie* made up a *gruppo*.

In the RAF and Commonwealth Air Forces the squadron of 9-12 aircraft constituted the basic fighter unit.

44

Left: **Tomahawk Mk II of SAAF No 5 Squadron 'somewhere in the desert'.** */IWM*

Below left: **Lt Chadwick of the SAAF returns his Tomahawk to Landing Ground 122 minus some of its essential operating parts following an air battle with Bf109s.** */Frank Smith via Ernie McDowell*

Right: **Air Vice Marshal Coningham talks with Sqn Ldr Caldwell during a visit to RAF No 112 Squadron.** */IWM*

Below: **A No 112 Squadron Kittyhawk at LG91, 1943.** */Frank Smith via Ernie McDowell*

pied with a long campaign against Malta which, though repeatedly mauled the brave little isle, never neutralised it for long.

During the summer and autumn of 1941, prior to Operation Crusader, the Desert Air Force squadrons equipped with Tomahawks had not only established good combat records, but, more importantly, had played a leading role in delineating, for the first time in World War II, some basic rules in the proper use of tactical air power. These were rules originally forumlated two decades earlier by Britain's Gen H. M. 'Boom' Trenchard and America's Gen Billy Mitchell. (Actually, Mitchell's basic tenets came from Trenchard. In his *Memoirs of World War I* (Random House, NYC, 1960) Mitchell quoted Trenchard's theories on air strategy and tactics and endorsed them without reservation.) Writing about the desert air war, RAF Grp Capt J. E. Johnson (38 confirmed air victories) said in *Full Circle; The Tactics of Air Fighting* (Ballantine Books, NYC, 1964):

'The fighter-bomber (what Trenchard called a bomb-loaded fighter) was the only suitable type of aeroplane for bombing and strafing whenever enemy fighters were about. It was known that the battlefield must be isolated to stop the enemy from moving into, and within, the combat area. It was known that the fighting men on the ground wanted close air support at the right time and right place, and that the whole thing depended

upon confidence between airman and soldier. Unfortunately, that close, intimate contact between soldier and airman in the First War had been lost, and it was not found again until the Eighth Army and the Desert Air Force got together.'

Tedder, and his Air Vice Marshals Coningham and (later) Broadhurst, worked closely with their counterparts on the ground. First-class communications was the key, and when RAF personnel began riding in the 8th Army's armoured cars in the battle zone, in direct radio contact with Desert Air Force fighters airborne in the area, close air support became about as close as it was possible to make it.

The Tomahawk, as a 'bomb-loaded fighter', surely would have warmed the heart of Boom

Trenchard. It was rugged, manoeuvrable, an able bomb carrier and a very good fighter at medium and low altitudes – good enough to produce a surprising number of aces over the western desert despite the fact that it was primarily employed in a ground support role.

The leading Hawk ace in North Africa was Australian Clive Caldwell, known as 'Killer' Caldwell, a sobriquet he himself was not particularly fond of. Plt Off Caldwell got his first air victory, a Messerschmitt Bf109E, on 26 June 1941, when nine Tomahawks of No 250 Squadron tangled with 30 Bf109s and Fiat G50s west of Capuzzo. The Tomahawks traded two of their own for three of the enemy that day. Four days later, Plt Off Caldwell shot down two Ju87 Stukas and shared a Bf110 with Sgt Plt Whittle while three addi-

tional enemy aircraft went down under the guns of other Tomahawks. Three Hawks were damaged.

Caldwell accounted for a Fiat G50 before that day in late August when, northwest of Sidi Barrani, a sharp Bf109 pilot gave him a short course in air fighting which punctured Caldwell's Tomahawk with more than 100 rounds of 7.9mm slugs, plus five 20mm cannon strikes. However, despite a shoulder wound, and flames streaking from his engine compartment, Caldwell shot down a Messerschmitt and then succeeded in starving the fire with a violent slip. He then nursed his flying wreck back to base at Sidi Haneish.

Back in action on 5 December with the rank of Flt Lt, Caldwell destroyed five Stukas and damaged a Fiat G50 when 22 Tomahawks of Nos 250 and 112 Squadrons attacked approximately 45 Stukas with 30 escorting fighters south of El Edem. Another six Stukas were shot down by other Tomahawk pilots, and seven of the enemy fighters – Bf109Fs and G50s – were claimed as damaged.

Caldwell was given command of No 112 Squadron in January 1942, and eventually logged 550 hours in Tomahawks and Kittyhawks while increasing his score to $20\frac{1}{2}$ enemy aircraft destroyed before going to the Southwest Pacific to fly Spitfires. He ended the war as a much-decorated group captain with $28\frac{1}{2}$ victories, ninth on the British list of aces.

Other Hawk aces of the desert war included Lt-Col Andrew C. Bosman, $10\frac{1}{2}$ victories, and Maj D. W. Golding, 10 victories, of the

South African Air Force. There were eventually five SAAF Hawk Squadrons, Nos 2, 4, 5, 10 and 11, although SAAF No 10 Squadron remained at Durban, South Africa, for sub hunting and shipping patrols, and No 11 Squadron, formed on Kittyhawks in mid-1944, fought in Italy.

South Africans were also predominant on the personnel roster of RAF No 250 Squadron, a truly cosmopolitan outfit, with pilots from Rhodesia, Australia, New Zealand, Canada, India, Malaya, the United Kingdom, Norway, some Free French and one American. The American was Sgt Plt A. F. Nitz, a Michigan native who had earlier joined the RCAF. Nitz later transferred to the USAAF as a captain.

The South African squadrons, as all others

fighting the desert war, moved often to various landing grounds, most so primitive and temporary that they bore no names but were simply numbers on a grid-map of that vast area. In June 1942, as Rommel pushed the British back into Egypt, SAAF No 2 Squadron occupied eight different landing grounds, while No 5 Squadron flew from seven. Throughout most of the desert war, home to the airmen was simply some spot or other in the desert.

Kittyhawks arrived in the western desert late in December 1941, and RAF Nos 250 and 112 Squadrons were re-equipped with these machines in January 1942. SAAF Nos 2 and 4 Squadrons received Kittyhawks in May 1942, but No 5 Squadron did not switch to Kittyhawks until the following January. RAAF No 450 Squadron on Malta also had Kittyhawks by that time. RAAF No 3 Squadron, with the Desert Air Force, had Kittyhawks by mid-1942. Perhaps we should again mention that the RAF and Commonwealth air forces called the P-40D and all subsequent P-40s 'Kittyhawks', while the USAAF called the P-40F and all subsequent P-40s 'Warhawks'.

Rommel's big offensive aginst the British was a two-stage operation. During January 1942 he forced the British back as far as Gazala in north-east Libya. Then in May, re-supplied and confident, he began the drive that would take his forces all the way to El Alamein, only 60 miles west of Alexandria in Egypt, by 1 July. There the British dug in, their right flank anchored at the tiny village of El Alamein on the sea, their left flank secured by the 200 miles of impassable salt marsh known as the Quattara Depression. Linking these points was the 30-mile Rueweisat Ridge, below which the British planted half-a-million land mines.

Rommel could not breach such a strong defensive position, although he made three attempts, the last one ending in September with the bloody battle of Adam El Halfa. By that time, Prime Minister Churchill had sent General Bernard Montgomery to Egypt

Right: **Combat art on Kittyhawk of RAAF No 450 Squadron.**
/*Frank Smith via Ernie McDowell*

Below: **This No 112 Squadron Kittyhawk bellied-in at Sidi Hanish 30 May 1942 during the retreat of the British into Egypt.**
/*Frank Smith via Ernie McDowell*

Left: **In January 1943, as Rommel retreated across Libya, visitors to the US 57th FG were (from left to right) Air Vice Marshal Coningham, Sir Sholto Douglas and Grp Capt Carter.**/*Col Archie Knight*

to take command of the British and Commonwealth forces there and defeat Rommel once and for all.

Meanwhile, in August, the USAAF 57th FG arrived in Palestine equipped with P-40Fs and Ks. This group contained the 64th, 65th and 66th FSs and, along with the USAAF 12th Medium Bomb Group then at Devesoir near Suez, formed the US Desert Air Task Force under Gen Lewis Brereton who had just come from India. These two American air groups would be totally committed to the air offensive against the Germans and Italians during the coming Battle of El Alamein. Actually, they were part of the new US 9th Air Force which Brereton had been ordered to put together with whatever US aircraft and personnel he could lay hands on – by whatever means. The US 9th Air Force would be part of Air Chief Marshal Tedder's Mediterranean Air Command, which was, of course, responsible to Gen Montgomery.

The sometimes tactless Montgomery has not been Britain's most beloved military leader, but he did grasp the proper use of air power long before the exigencies of modern warfare forced these concepts upon other top Allied generals. The air strategy and tactics employed by Montgomery resulted from the thinking (and persuasive powers) of Tedder and Air Vice Marshal Coningham; but the point is, Montgomery recognised the soundness of his air commanders' dogma and acted upon it. Coningham's planes first gained control of the air over Egypt, then, at El Alamein and in the weeks that followed, were able to exploit that control by effectively performing the other, now classic tasks required of tactical air forces. The American air intelligence officer on Brereton's staff,

Lt-Col Cornelius V. Whitney wrote, in *Lone and Level Sands* (Farrar, Straus and Young Inc, NYC 1951): 'For the first time, we saw clearly the role of air power in modern warfare . . .'

On the eve of the Battle of El Alamein Whitney's official estimate, based on information provided by RAF air intelligence, listed relative fighter strengths as 160 German, 380 Italian, 544 British and 63 American. The German fighters were Bf109s; the British and Commonwealth fighters included six Kittyhawk squadrons (others were equipped with Hurricanes and Spitfires), and the American fighters were represented by the three squadrons of Warhawks of the 57th FG. In November and December 1942, two additional US Warhawk-equipped fighter groups, the 79th and 324th, would reach Egypt to join the Desert Air Force. By that time, almost half of all Allied fighters in the western desert were Kittyhawks or Warhawks.

Montgomery opened his offensive at El Alamein on the night of 23 October 1942, and during the 12 days following, until units of the 8th Army at last breached Rommel's defences and the Afrika Korps began its long retreat towards final defeat, the Desert Air Force flew an incredible number of close support missions which directly contributed to the victory. General Montgomery put it this way in *Alamein and the Desert War* (Ballantine Books, NYC, 1968; Ed Derek Jewell): 'It is not too much to say that without the air power which supported the land forces, the battle could not have been won in 12 days, if at all. The action of the Desert Air Force and Tedder's bombers was beyond all praise.'

The South African Air Force squadrons, which had done their share earlier in the year

To All Arab Peoples — Greetings and Peace be upon you. The bearer of this letter is an Officer of the British Government and a friend of all Arabs. Treat him well, guard him from harm, give him food and drink, help him to return to the nearest British soldiers and you will be rewarded. Peace and the Mercy of God upon you. *The British High Command in the East.*

SOME POINTS ON CONDUCT WHEN MEETING THE ARABS IN THE DESERT.

Remove footwear on entering their tents. Completely ignore their women. If thirsty drink the water they offer, but DO NOT fill your waterbottle from their personal supply. Go to their well and fetch what you want. Never neglect any puddle or other water supply for topping up your bottle. Use the Halazone included in your Aid Box. Do not expect breakfast if you sleep the night. Arabs will give you a mid-day or evening meal.

REMEMBER, NEVER TRY AND HURRY IN THE DESERT, SLOW AND SURE DOES IT.

A few useful words

English	Arabic		English	Arabic
English	Ingleezi		Day	Nahaar or Yom
Friend	Sa-hib, Sa-deck.		Night	Layl
Water	Moya		Half	Nuss
Food	Akl		Half a day	Nuss il Nahaar
Village	Balaad		Near	Gareeb
Tired	Ta-eban		Far	Baeed
Take me to the English and you will be rewarded.			{ Hud nee eind el Ingleez wa tahud	
			Mu-ka-fa.	
English Flying Officer	Za-bit Ingleezi Tye-yara			
How far (how many kilos?)	Kam kilo ?			
Enemy	Germani, Taliani, Siziliani			

Distance and time: Remember, Slow & Sure does it

The older Arabs cannot read, write or tell the time. They measure distance by the number of days journey. "Near" may mean 10 minutes or 10 hours. Far probably means over a days journey. A days journey is probably about 30 miles. The younger Arabs are more accurate.

GOOD LUCK

Above: **Letter issued to pilots of the Desert Air Force to aid their return if downed in the desert.**/*Col Archie Knight*

to whittle down enemy air opposition, were held in reserve and did not participate in the Battle of El Alamein, but were back in action from Landing Ground 97 in the desert by 9 November. RAF Nos 250 and 112 Squadrons, along with RAAF No 3 Squadron, were the Kittyhawk squadrons that fought over El Alamein with the US 57th FGs Warhawks. Other Desert Air Force fighters committed were RAF Spits, Hurricanes (which specialised in tank-busting) and Beaufighters.

'Tedder's bombers', as Montgomery characterised them, included B-17s, B-24s, and B-25s of Brereton's US 9th Air Force, SAAF A-20s and RAF 'Wimpys' (Wellingtons).

A typical action for the 57th FGs Warhawks during the battle was on 26 October when 16 aircraft of the 64th and 65th FSs encountered a large formation of Stukas, protected (more or less) by Fiat CR42 fighters.

The Warhawk pilots destroyed seven of the enemy, counted three probables and damaged three others without loss to themselves. By 4 November, when the first units of the 8th Army began their breakout at El Alamein, the American squadrons had a total of 20 confirmed air victories in addition to their assigned bombing and strafing missions in close support of the ground forces. During the battle, Caldwell's RAF No 112 Squadron operated with the American 66th FS.

Torrential rains on 6 and 7 November allowed Rommel to organise his retreat, sow mines in his wake and set up delaying rearguard actions free of constant attack by the Desert Air Force. However, late on the 7th Rommel learned of the Allied landings in north-west Africa and the Desert Fox knew that there would be no firm stand at a place of his choosing while he re-fitted and prepared a counter-attack. He no longer had only the British 8th Army to deal with – in itself more than he could handle without substantial re-supply from across the Mediterranean – but now faced another army closing on him from the opposite direction. Writing in his diary Rommel seems bitter about the unrelenting pressure put upon him by the Desert Air Force, but he assesses no blame for it. Apparently, the German high command was giving him all the air support it felt it could afford.

In any case, the air action in the desert war was mostly at medium and low altitudes where either the Kittyhawk or Warhawk was easily a match for the Bf109F. True, the Messerschmitt had a superior weight-to-horsepower ratio, but this showed up only in a better climb rate, and few Kittyhawk/Warhawk pilots would trade their craft's extra weight (read that 'ruggedness') for the Bf109's superior climb. Speeds below 15,000ft were approximately the same, and the Kittyhawk/Warhawk was at least as manoeuvrable as the aircraft Clive Caldwell described as 'over-rated'.

The top speeds of the Curtisses ranged from the Tomahawk's 345mph to 378mph for the P-40N/Kittyhawk Mk IV. The Kittyhawk Mk IA then in service with the Desert Air Force had a maximum speed of 354mph at 15,000ft, an initial climb rate of 2,580ft/min and its gross weight was 8,800lb. The P-40Ks of the 57th FG were a few miles per hour faster, 800lb heavier fully loaded and paid for it with a 2,000ft/min climb rate.

The Bf109F had a maximum speed of 380mph at 17,000ft, but only 320mph at sea level. This craft weighed but 6,000lb fully loaded and possessed a climb rate of 3,600ft/min initially. The first Bf109G models reached North Africa in October 1942, during the Battle of El Alamein, and although this machine could attain a speed of 400mph at

50

21,000ft, at sea level this dropped to 325mph. The G model was 700lb heavier than the Bf109F, and less manoeuvrable.

The principal Italian fighters in North Africa were the Macchi C200 and C202. The C200 was in the Hawk 75 (Mohawk) class and the C202 was barely a match for the early Tomahawks. The Italian fighters, however, were highly manoeuvrable and Caldwell later said (in a letter to the authors) he believed the C202 would have been superior to the Bf109 had it possessed sufficient power.

As a practical matter, over North Africa, the advantage held by the Bf109 pilot was his ability to get up high, make a diving pass at the Curtiss pilot and zoom back to altitude. Even this tactic was largely nullified if the Kittyhawk or Warhawk pilot was aware of the attack and turned into his attacker to meet him head on at the proper moment. Should the Messerschmitt pilot elect to hang around and dogfight the Curtiss at low altitude then he should be considered the disadvantaged one, pilot ability being equal.

Pilot ability. There, so often, lay the deciding factor. And it would be highly unfair to the Allied pilots who met the Luftwaffe fighters in combat if we fail to recognise this factor. The German fighter pilot was aggressive, intelligent and well trained, especially early in the war. Many had fought with the Condor Legion in Spain during the late 1930s. Also, the German fighter pilot was not normally retired from combat after a given number of missions or victories, but remained a combat pilot as long as the war lasted or until he was killed or could no longer fly. This is why more than 100 of them could claim 100 or more air victories at war's end.

The relatively poorer showing of the Italians has generally been attributed to two principal causes: their machines were obsolescent at best and they were poorly motivated. Like the Vichy French, not many were keen about fighting the British and Americans.

By 15 November 1942 the 57th FG and RAF No 112 Squadron were temporarily flying from the Gambut Airfields in Libya, awaiting the rehabilitation of the field at Gazula. RAF No 250 Squadron was at Gazala with the SAAF Kittyhawk squadrons. All continued to harass the retreating Germans and Italians, the main enemy forces being somewhere between Benghazi and Agedabia with Montgomery pursuing rather cautiously some 200 miles behind at Derna.

From that time until the war in North Africa ended six months later, Desert Air Force fighter squadrons moved so frequently it seems pointless to list all the landing grounds and airfields from which they operated in Libya.

On 20 November Rommel halted to make a stand at El Agheila, about halfway across

Libya, but on 12 December the British smashed through his outposts there and flanked him to the south so the Afrika Korps retreated to Buerat where the same action took place all over again in mid-January 1943. The Desert Fox had exhausted his bag of tricks. At the end of January he retreated into Tunisia, linked up with the German and Italian forces which were fighting Eisenhower's army, and established a strong defensive position facing Montgomery along the Mareth Line, a 20-mile long system of hardened emplacements built by the French before the war to prevent Italian incursion into Tunisia.

A detailed account of the Hawk squadrons' operations during the pursuit of Rommel into Tunisia quickly becomes repetitive. RAF No 250 Squadron records reveal that this unit was paying particular attention to Rommel's aerial supply line from Sicily, and its air victories included seven Ju52/53s, nine He111Ds and a Caproni C311D, plus a Ju88 and a number of enemy aircraft destroyed on the ground although not identified. To break the monotony, Sgt Nitz, after shooting down two Junkers transports, found some German troops lined up at a field kitchen so Nitz dived to the deck and added one German field kitchen to his tally that day. That was especially satisfying to a pilot who himself hadn't enjoyed a hot meal for days.

Meanwhile, the SAAF Nos 2, 4 and 5 Squadrons were at Martuba from where they alternately flew low-level fighter sweeps and fighter-bomber missions. Desert Air Force Spitfires were usually on hand at high altitude to accost the relatively few enemy fighters that appeared during this time. SAAF No 5 Squadron was still flying Tomahawks through December 1942.

Above: **Capt George D. Hobbs of the 57th FG was wounded by cannon fire from a Bf109 but returned to base in Libya in this P-40K-1.**/*USAF*

51

Above left: **In the desert, a wing-sitter was normally used as an extra pair of eyes while taxying.**/*Don Berlin*

Left: **A 324th FG Warhawk at Deversoir, Egypt early in 1943.**/*USAF*

Above right: **An RAF No 250 Squadron Kittyhawk bearing 'routine' battle damage.** /*USAF*

Below: **P-40F Warhawks of the 57th FG in Egypt at the time of Montgomery's breakout at El Alamein.** /*USAF*

4 Operation Torch and Italy

Three days after the Battle of El Alamein began, British and American ships – 650 in all – put to sea bound for north-west Africa laden with troops and equipment to invade French-held Morocco and Algeria. This army, commanded by Gen Dwight D. Eisenhower, expected to move swiftly eastward into Tunisia to crush Rommel between it and the British 8th Army which was chasing the Germans and Italians from the opposite direction.

All of which was easier planned than accomplished. There was far more fight left in the Desert Fox than the Allies then imagined; and Eisenhower apparently had a lot to learn about military logistics and the proper use of air power.

D-Day for Operation Torch was 8 November 1942, by which time Rommel's forces were withdrawing from Siddi Barrani in north-west Egypt. The Allied invasion force landed at several points around Oran, Algiers and at Port Lyautey, Safi, and Fedhala around Casablanca, Morocco. Supporting navy forces included the US Navy Task Group 34, with its air groups operating from a fleet carrier and three escort carriers. A fourth escort carrier, the CVE *Chenango*, had her decks full of the 33rd FGs P-40 Warhawks.

On 11 November the confused French threw down their arms (following a marathon parley behind the scenes with several French commanders) and other Allied aircraft began to trickle into Moroccan and Algerian landing grounds. Among these air units were the 1st and 14th FGs, equipped with P-38s. HMS *Archer* also brought 25 additional Warhawks for the 33rd FG. Meanwhile, most of the Allied air cover was supplied by Spitfires from Gibralter and from US Navy fighters from Task Group 34.

The authors are aware of at least one report which describes a great air battle on the first day of the invasion between US Navy F4F Wildcats (Martlets) and the Hawk 75s flown by the French Groupes I/5 at Rabat and II/5 at Casablanca, these units being among those that fled to North Africa when France fell 18 months earlier. However, search as we might, we were unable to find any official documentation for this confrontation which was said to have resulted in the downing of 14 French Hawks and eight Wildcats. Neither can we say that it did not happen. Noting the touchy political climate at the time, one is naturally left with the suspicion that both the Americans and the French would have been inclined to sweep such an incident under the carpet.

One such political shenanigan that does admit to official documentation was Eisenhower's decision to divert 25 P-40F Warhawks, badly needed by the 33rd FG, to the French II/5 Groupe just two weeks later. True, II/5 Groupe served honourably in the Allied cause over Tunisia – after two of its pilots 're-defected' to the Germans in their brand new Warhawks. All things considered it seems a shame that we couldn't have arranged for World War II to have been fought between the French and the Italians.

The three days that the Vichy-French (so called because the puppet government of occupied France sat in Vichy, France) chose to fight for their German masters imposed a significant delay upon the Allied invasion forces. The British and Americans regarded France as an ally in spirit if not in fact, and hoped there would be no resistance. The Allies were of course prepared to fight if necessary; but they were not prepared for the swift reaction of the Germans who began airlifting troops into Tunis on 9 November, only one day after the invasion began.

The airfields at Oran were captured on the 10th, and the 33rd FG flew its 70 P-40Fs from the *Chenango*'s decks to occupy those fields that same day. The 33rd FG was commanded by Col William 'Spike' Momyer, and its three squadrons were the 58th, 59th and 60th. The 33rd, which entered combat immediately, was part of Gen Jimmy Doolittle's US 12th Air Force, most of which had staged through Gibraltar for the invasion.

The 325th FG would follow in January as the second Warhawk-equipped group in the newly formed 12th Air Force, but these pilots were obliged to give up their aircraft to the (by then) decimated 33rd FG, so the 325th was unable to enter combat until

April 1943. Two additional Warhawk groups, the 79th and 324th, reached Egypt in November and December, respectively, to join the US 9th Air Force and the veteran 57th FG fighting with Montgomery. In February 1943 all US Warhawk groups would be re-assigned to the US 12th Air Force which, along with British air units in north-west Africa, would make up the North-west African Air Forces (NAAF) under US Gen Carl 'Tooey' Spaatz. The NAAF was part of the Mediterranean Air Command headed by Air Chief Marshal Tedder. Air Vice Marshal Coningham was boss of the fighters.

This reorganisation came about as a result of Eisenhower's failure to reach Tunis before Christmas. Operation Torch had sputtered along from the beginning. Although the censored press reports from North Africa at the time made Torch sound like a resounding success, the truth was, in both planning and execution, the operation was poorly handled. Quite simply, the Americans were unprepared for the endless seas of mud that came with the winter rains. They were unprepared for the Germans' ability to quickly move an army of seasoned troops into the area. Indeed, the Allies were even without the ability to supply adequately the 157,000 men in

Eisenhower's forces once the initial thrust of Operation Torch had spent itself. Add to those handicaps the fact that Eisenhower soon had his limited tactical fighter forces scattered over 600 miles of north-west Africa to serve, piecemeal, the presumed needs of local ground commanders; and the fact that he did not possess a photo-recce squadron until after his advance was stalled in December by a combination of the above-mentioned factors.

Then, on 14 February, Rommel unexpectedly struck at poorly deployed US troops in the mountains of Central Tunisia, and although the Afrika Korps withdrew after gaining Kasserine Pass, they took 2,000 American prisoners with them.

A week later, Britain's Field Marshal Sir Harold Alexander took command of the entire front and, with Tedder in charge of all Allied air forces in North Africa, the situation began to improve.

Meanwhile, the richly experienced Desert Air Force, having harried Rommel all the way across Libya, was strong and fit and able to contribute four Warhawk groups – the 57th, 79th, 324th and 325th – to the NAAF for the Tunisian Campaign while its SAAF Kittyhawk squadrons, Nos 2, 4 and 5, along with its RAF and RAAF Kittyhawk squad-

Above: **At about the time Churchill and Roosevelt were meeting in Casablanca the US was presenting 25 P-40F Warhawks to former Vichy French pilots at Maison Blanche Aerodrome.**
/National Archives

rons continued to press Rommel from the east.

The 33rd FG, which had been under Eisenhower's command, had only 13 flyable Warhawks remaining after the Battle of Kasserine Pass, and the French II/5 Groupe had but five. The two P-38 Lightning groups had suffered comparable losses. Flying (when possible) from the mud of unprepared air-fields and committed in small numbers to bomber escort and ground-attack missions against local targets and under skies in which the German fighters operated at will, the fighter strength of the US 12th Air Force had been frittered away to relatively small gain. Properly directed, however, they too would soon establish enviable records.

The authors do not intend the above as an indictment of Gen Eisenhower. Clearly, he did not select himself as commander of Operation Torch. This decision had to be shared by Prime Minister Churchill and President Roosevelt, and almost certainly was a political determination. Militarily it appears obvious that these leaders would have better served their common cause – and those whose lives for which they were responsible – had they chosen the highly-experienced Alexander in the first place. Eisenhower did profit greatly from his on-the-job training in North Africa, but at high cost.

Perhaps it is appropriate to mention, as Gen Montgomery repeatedly pointed out, that even the best commanders and the soundest of plans must ultimately depend upon the men who do the fighting for whatever success is achieved.

In the 57th FG, Maj Archie Knight was one of those who did the fighting, an example of which took place early in March 1943 as the NAAF was concentrating (at last) on taking control of the air over Northern Tunisia. On this day, 16 Warhawks en route to bomb a German airfield were just turning inland from their sea approach when approximately 25 Bf109s came diving down upon them. Major Knight and his section turned into the attacking enemy. Col (ret) Knight recalls:

'The air was so full of planes it reminded me of a cadet centre. My section and I drew blood with our first bursts as I saw three of the oncoming aircraft pull away leaving heavy smoke trails indicating they had run into our concentrated fire. I'm afraid it was an even trade as I could hear the metallic "clink" when several rounds from the enemies' guns entered my fuselage in the nose section. A second or two later I became aware of the definite odour of my coolant and correctly judged that I had been hit in the glycol tank.

'I spun down out of the fight and as I recovered from the spin I saw an American plane under attack by one of the enemy. I dived on the Messerschmitt, gave him one long burst from my guns and saw my tracers entering his fuselage at the wing root. The German half-rolled and plunged into the sea in the inverted position.

'By this time my engine was so hot I thought it might explode any instant, so there was nothing to do but cut the switches and salvage some sort of forced landing from the situation. You know a fighter doesn't have the best gliding qualities in the world, and I was too low to parachute.

'I chose a narrow arm of land that jutted into the sea as it seemed the most removed from the flashes on the ground denoting German infantry positions. Luckily, the land itself was rather marsh-like and the plane bellied in with a small amount of swerving and bumping. I guess those next few minutes were the busiest of my life as the Germans had my range and started to shell my little beach. Using a Boy Scout knife that I carried largely for sentimental reasons, I dug into the moist earth faster than a power-dredge could have scooped a similar trench.

'As soon as twilight fell I managed to wade, swim, and float across nearly 10 miles of open water to the British positions. Oddly enough, a British pilot forced down on the same spot just two days later was taken prisoner by a German patrol.'

Maj Knight, who was operations officer for the 57th FG, was officially credited with one enemy aircraft destroyed and two damaged in the above action, and was made a member in good standing of the 'Late Arrivals Club', an organisation comprised of pilots who walked (or swam) back to safety after being forced down in the desert.

By late March Tedder's airmen controlled the air over the entire Mediterranean Theatre of Operations (MTO), and the North-west African Air Forces ruled their share of it.

Above: **This photo, dated May 1943, apparently establishes that the French still had at least eight H75-A2s and A-3s at Marrakech Aerodrome (Morocco) as of that date.** /*USAF*

Left: **Maj Archie Knight, Ops Officer of the 57th FG.**

On 7 April the British 8th Army, having out-flanked the Germans on the Mareth Line, linked up with the US II Corps in Central Tunisia. The two armies, which had started out nearly 2,000 miles apart, had closed the jaws of their giant pincer and now had the enemy in North Africa surrounded and backed against the sea.

Since the blockade by the British Navy had long since denied meaningful supply to the Axis armies in Africa by sea, the enemy had assembled a large fleet of transport aircraft which, during the four months December to March inclusive, ferried more than 40,000 men and 14,000 tons of supplies from Italy, by way of Sicily, to Tunisia. This was the enemy's last tenuous lifeline, and it was bared to the Allied air forces when the Luftwaffe was defeated over Tunisia. It

would be almost completely severed with a single blow.

It happened on Palm Sunday, 18 April 1943, and that action has been known ever since as the 'Palm Sunday Massacre'. That is an apt description, because late that after-noon off Cape Bon, 46 Warhawks, with 12 RAF Spitfires flying top cover, destroyed 75 aircraft in a one-sided 10-minute air battle.

All that day, NAAF and Desert Air Force fighters had been patrolling the sea looking for the German transports. The 79th FG had searched that morning, and again in the early afternoon, followed by RAF and SAAF Spits and Kittyhawks. All had found nothing. Then at 1650 hours it was the turn of the 57th FGs three squadrons (64th, 65th and 66th), 34 machines in all, with 12 Warhawks from the 324th FGs 314th Squadron tagging

Below: **Crew of 64th FS, 57th FG arm a Warhawk prior to a mission.**/*Col Archie Knight*

Bottom: **P-40F-15s and F-20s of the 325th FG at Maison Blanche.**/*USAF*

along for what would apparently be an evening joyride.

The 46 Warhawks, flying from their base at El Djem, rendezvoused over Hergla with the Spitfires and, led by Capt Curl of the 66th FS, headed out to sea flying four abreast and stair-stepped upwards between 4,000 and 12,000ft. The Spitfires, led by Kittyhawk ace Sqn Ldr Neville Duke, were at 15,000ft just below an overcast.

The official Intelligence Summary of what followed is typically emotionless:
'. . . skirted coast to Naboul, then NW to K-3060, then NE along coast to K-5080 where 100-plus tri-motored transports were encountered (some Savois, but mostly Ju52s) flying on deck in NE direction escorted by 30-plus Bf109s and Bf110s flying from 4,000ft down to deck. Enemy aircraft were engaged.'

The grid number K-5080 was approximately six miles west of Cape Bon, roughly opposite Ras El Ahmar, over the Gulf of Tunis. The Ju52s were in three Vs of 30 or more aircraft each, were painted in gray, blue and green camouflage that blended well into the water beneath, and as the Hawks fell upon them they turned shoreward.

The Intelligence Summary continues:
'Some e/a are believed to have bellied in at K-8090 which apparently is a LG. Many a/c, 20 to 40 Jus, were seen to belly land on beach at K-7693 (near Cape Bon), Between 50 and 60 fires were observed in vicinity of beach. A considerable number of personnel, many believed to be troops, were reported by pilots to have leaped out of crashed a/c that bellied in.

'The pilots of the Bf109s were considered to have flown their a/c in a confused and inferior fashion after the engagement began, possibly due to the low altitude. In the engagement, many personnel, possibly troops, were observed firing with tommy guns from the Ju52s. Pilots report rear stingers in some of the Ju52s. One four-engine a/c was observed in the Ju52 formation. 80% of the Ju52s destroyed are estimated to have been

flamers and very few transports, if any, left the target area.

'One Warhawk pilot, believed to be Lt Blakely of 65th Squadron, bailed out at K-6885 and his a/c hit the water at K-6284. Pilots of Warhawks are reported to have bailed out at K-6595 and K-4580. It cannot be determined whether this is a duplication of other reports. A Warhawk bellied in at F-0090. The pilot was seen swimming in the water. Lt Cleveland of 66th Squadron suffered a broken arm on landing. His a/c Cat #3. Lt Ottoway of 64th Squadron and Lt Stahl of 66th Squadron landed at other LGs and are safe. Three pilots of 314th Squadron are missing, namely: Capt Phillips last heard on the R/T reporting gas low; Lt Bicksler and Lt Werner about whom nothing is known. Three pilots of the 65th Squadron are missing, namely: Lt Costanza, Lt Randall, and Lt Blakely. Nothing is known about the first two; but Lt Blakely is believed to have bailed out at K-6590 noted above. 10/10 clouds at 15,000ft. Visibility poor. 25,000 rounds of ammunition were expended. (46 sorties.)

'Note: This organisation realises the tremendously important part played by 244 Wing in our last mission of the day. For the splendid cover provided and the job of keeping enemy fighters occupied throughout the battle, although greatly outnumbered, go our heartiest thanks.'

This report concludes with a list of enemy aircraft destroyed and damaged by each Warhawk pilot. The totals came to 58 Ju52s, 14 Bf109s, and two Bf110s destroyed; one Bf109 is listed as a probable, and 19 Ju52s, nine Bf109s, and one Bf110 were claimed as damaged. Two Warhawk pilots, Lt Cleveland of the 66th FS, and Lt Duffey of the 314th, accounted for five Ju52s each. Eight others destroyed three enemy aircraft each.

Maj Knight? It seems that he elected not to assign himself to the evening patrol that day in order to catch up on some paperwork. Along with a couple of other 57th FG veterans who had traded their places on the mission

Below: **The 86th FS, 79th FG was at Gambut Aerodrome in Libya early in 1943.**
/*Frank F. Smith*

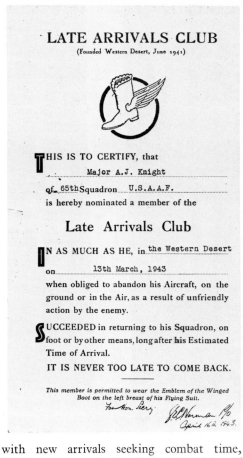

LATE ARRIVALS CLUB
(Founded Western Desert, June 1941)

THIS IS TO CERTIFY, that

Major A.J. Knight

of 65th Squadron U.S.A.A.F.

is hereby nominated a member of the

Late Arrivals Club

IN AS MUCH AS HE, in the Western Desert

on 13th March, 1943

when obliged to abandon his Aircraft, on the ground or in the Air, as a result of unfriendly action by the enemy.

SUCCEEDED in returning to his Squadron, on foot or by other means, long after his Estimated Time of Arrival.

IT IS NEVER TOO LATE TO COME BACK.

This member is permitted to wear the Emblem of the Winged Boot on the left breast of his Flying Suit.

with new arrivals seeking combat time, Knight was strongly impelled to kick himself around the airfield a few times as he listened to the exultant R/T chatter of his returning pilots. A total of 75 enemy aircraft destroyed in exchange for six Warhawks; that would go into the history books, he reflected. He was right.

The Spitfires, by the way, while dutifully leaving the Jus to the Warhawks and concentrating on keeping the Messerschmitts busy, could claim but one enemy aircraft destroyed, although the true measure of the Spits' performance was reflected in the fact that only six Warhawks were lost in the battle.

Twice more during the next four days the enemy attempted to slip 20-plane formations of Me323s into Tunisia, but lost 12 of them on the 19th and all 20 of them – along with 10 fighters – on the 22nd. The Warhawks of the 79th FG shared in these victories, as did the Spits of No 244 Wing and the Kittyhawks of SAAF No 5 Squadron. Then, when in desperation the Germans tried to slip in some transports at night, Desert Air Force night Beaufighters were waiting. Rommel's last hope for supply by air was gone.

By early May, the stubborn enemy was forced from the Tunisian hills, and on 13 May 1943 270,000 Axis troops pinned on the Cape Bon Peninsula surrendered. Field Marshal Rommel and a relative handful of Afrika Korps officers flew to Sicily and Italy shortly before the end.

During the last days of the fighting in Tunisia, two squadrons of the Warhawk-equipped 325th FG entered combat. The 318th and 319th FSs flew about 20 missions before the 317th Squadron received its planes. The 325th FG had been formed in the US 10 months earlier from a cadre of 79th FG personnel, had flown its Warhawks from the Fleet Carrier *Ranger* to Tafaraoui, Algiers in January, but then had its aircraft taken away to re-equip the French II/5 Groupe. Not until 17 April was it able to fly its first mission, and the war in North Africa was over by the time the 325th reached full strength.

However, Pantelleria, Sardinia, and Sicily remained, as well as Italy itself, and the 325th 'Checkertails' had plenty of time to distinguish themselves.

Another late arrival in North Africa was the 99th FS. At the time, it belonged to no group. Its personnel was black. Its Warhawks were P-40Ns, and its commander Col Benjamin O. Davis, Jr, the first black officer in 47 years to graduate from the US Military Academy. The 99th received theatre indoctrination in Morocco, and moved up to El Aouina Airfield near Tunis for its first combat mission on 2 June 1943.

The 99th participated in the aerial subjugation of Pantelleria, an Axis island base in the Mediterranean some 40 miles off Cape Bon, which became the first bit of enemy territory conquered entirely by airpower. The black fighter pilots possessed no dinghies, only Mae Wests, so the return flight from a bomb/strafe mission to Pantelleria, and later Sicily, was viewed by them with some apprehension. After a time, however, this faded as they came to appreciate the Warhawk's ability to absorb punishment and still fly. 'We grew to believe that nobody could hurt us in a P-40,' Col Davis said later. 'We'd always stay with the aircraft and crash-land rather than bail-out, unless we were on fire.'

Davis, who later became a general and commanded the US 13th Air Force, went on to say that the German fighters usually refused to dogfight his Warhawks. The Bf109s and the Fw190s that were then appearing in the MTO, made diving attacks and zoomed back to altitude out of range of the Warhawks. 'If they ever came down and fought us below 15,000ft we'd tear them up and they knew it,' the General said. 'The P-40L was a better all-round fighter in its own element.' (From a personal interview following dedication of the Benjamin O. Davis Senior Citizens' Center, Lawton, OK, August 1970.)

As Allied air power began softening up Sicily for invasion, the 99th's principal mis-

sion was that of escorting 12th Air Force B-25 Mitchells, the crews of which probably never knew that the friendly Warhawks above were manned by America's first black fighter pilots.

Davis returned to the US in October 1943 to form the all Negro 332nd FG which fought in Italy and Greece with P-39s and P-47s. The 99th FS joined the group in June 1944. This four-squadron group, although chiefly assigned to ground-attack duties, officially destroyed 111 enemy aircraft in aerial combat.

The invasion of Sicily, Operation Husky, began on 10 July 1943 as 160,000 men of the British 8th Army and the US 7th Army landed on the southern and eastern coasts of that strategic island and began a 39-day march on Messina. The Allies took 31,000 casualties during the campaign, and although the Germans managed to evacuate under cover of darkness and with strong Luftwaffe support, this was the action that took Italy out of the war (officially announced on 8 September after the Mussolini government was overthrown), and the Allies found themselves looking just three miles across the Strait of Messina to the Italian mainland.

All the Hawk units of the NAAF and Desert

Above: **The fine desert dust created problems for all things mechanical including the guns in the Bf109s.**

Right: **America's top World War I ace, Capt Eddie Rickenbacker (right) with the 57th FG's Col Art Salisbury.**
/Col Archie Knight

Air Force, except the 325th FG, participated in the massive pre-invasion aerial assault on Sicily as well as the Battle of Sicily that followed. The Warhawks and Kittyhawks were much in evidence because the American groups, the 33rd, 57th, 79th and 324th, each with approximately 100 aircraft (36 per squadron), could count a total of roughly 400 machines, while SAAF Nos 4 and 5, RAF Nos 250, 260 and 112, plus RAAF Nos 3 and 450 Squadrons, all Kittyhawk-equipped, added an additional 100 or so. Since the remaining Allied fighter strength in the theatre consisted of nine RAF Spitfire

squadrons, one US group flying Spitfires (the 31st) and three US P-38 groups, nearly half of the Allied fighters were Warhawks or Kittyhawks. These figures don't include the 325th FG which stayed behind in Tunisia for a time charged with the task of smashing the enemy in Sardinia.

Air Marshal Tedder continued as boss of all Allied air in the theatre until the following November when, in Italy, the North-West African Air Forces and the Desert Air Force were merged into the Mediterranean Allied Air Forces (MAAF) commanded by US Gen Ira Eaker. Tedder and Coningham returned to England where their considerable talents were needed for the air war over northern Europe.

As quickly as enemy airfields were captured in Sicily, the Hawk units moved in and continued their role as tactical fighter-bombers, their missions divided between medium bomber escort and bomb/strafe attacks on enemy lines of communication and transport. It was a tough job, with a higher degree of risk than aerial combat, but with small chance for glory. The headlines back home went to the aces. Col Knight says:

'We were duly grateful, on those relatively rare occasions when 109s and 190s chose to come down and fight us. We could out-turn them, and out-dive them. Over Africa we often had superior firepower as well because of that powdery-fine dust that got into everything. It caused the Germans a great deal of trouble with their guns, particularly the cannon on the Bf109s. Those cannon were beautifully made and machined to close tolerances and the dust jammed them. That

Above: **Kittyhawk Mk IIIs (P-40K-1) of RAF No 260 Squadron in Libya, early 1943.**/*USAF*

Left: **P-40K-1s being assembled on a desert airfield previously occupied by the Italians.**/*USAF*

Below left: **Maintenance on the Merlin-powered Warhawks of the 57th FG in the Libyan desert.** /*Frank F. Smith*

left the enemy pilot with his rifle-calibre guns against our .50cals which perhaps were not as well made, had greater tolerances in the mechanisms and, as Lord Tedder once remarked, seemed to work better with dust in them.

'Tedder, by the way, was a remarkable man and a great air commander. He was a disciple of Slessor, you know. I don't know how Tedder did it, but he appeared to know by name every pilot in his command.'

Near the end of July, when a final assault against the Germans was being readied in Sicily, the Germans began to withdraw across the Strait of Messina. Despite constant air attacks by Allied aircraft some 60,000 of the enemy escaped to Italy before American troops pushed into Messina on 17 August.

The surrender of the Italians following the Axis defeat in Sicily had no great impact on the war in the MTO because the Germans had more than 20 divisions in Italy and intended to keep them there. The Allies would have but 11 divisions (the US 5th Army and British 8th Army), and would have to make up the difference with air power. The Hawk units as usual would be in the vanguard, striking at critical tactical targets, and as usual would be highly effective, but after the Allies were firmly established in Italy most of the Warhawk and Kittyhawk units were re-equipped with P-47s and, later, P-51s.

(Latter day photo identification may be

Above: Snifter **was a Kittyhawk Mk I (AK591) of RAAF No 3 Squadron.**
|Frank F Smith

Left: **Sgt Plt Dick Rowe of RAAF No 3 Squadron.**
|Frank F. Smith

aided if one is familiar with the fuselage identifier codes employed in the MTO. There were: SAAF No 2 Squadron, DB; No 4 Squadron, KJ, and No 5 Squadron, GL. RAF No 250 Squadron, LD; No 112 Squadron, GA, and No 260 Squadron, HS. RAAF No 450 Squadron, OK, and RAAF No 3 Squadron CV.)

The invasion of Italy began on 3 September when the British crosssed the Strait of Messina and landed on the toe of the Italian boot. Six days later, the Americans landed on the beaches along the Gulf of Salerno, while a British fleet steamed into the harbour of Taranto. After bitter fighting, especially in the Salerno area, the Americans took Naples two weeks later, and the British took

Foggia, the site of an extensive airfield complex.

As the invasion of Italy began, SAAF No 4 Squadron converted to Spitfires, but SAAF No 5 Squadron not only fought the Italian campaign in Kittyhawks – first from Taranto, then Foggia – but also took their Hawks to Crete in August 1944.

Three months later, in November 1944, SAAF No 29 Squadron, which had formed on Spitfires in July from SAAF No 11 Squadron Operational Training Squadron, converted to Kittyhawks at Perugia in north-central Italy, and was assigned the Kittyhawks' usual role of bomb/strafe missions along with some medium bomber escort duty. This unit was based at Udine in north-east Italy, still

Top: **Messerschmitt Bf109 forced down intact by pilots of the RAAF No 3 Squadron.** /*Frank F. Smith*

Above: **Kittyhawk IIIs of RAAF No 450 Squadron at Castel Benito, Libya early in 1943.**/*Frank F. Smith*

flying Kittyhawks, when the war ended in the ETO.

The US Warhawk groups in Italy kept their aircraft until early spring 1944, but the 325th Checkertails, which had remained behind in Tunisia, traded their Hawks for P-47s in September 1943, after spending a month softening up the island of Sardinia. The 325th FG was the only Allied fighter unit assigned to the task, but were so effective the group soon became known as the 'Sardinian Air Force'. As Capt John Watkins explained it in *Checkertail Clan* (Ernest R. McDowell and William N. Hess, Aero Publishers, Fallbrook, CA, 1969):

'Ours was strictly a gentlemen's war. We set our own time and place to fight. We ranged up and down the island, staging dogfights in the best Hollywood style when we – by dropping fragmentation bombs on enemy aerodromes – made them mad enough to come up and fight us. We dive-bombed power stations, bridges, and factories, strafed air raid warning stations along the coast, and enemy ships whenever one attempted a rare dash down the coast in daylight.'

The 325th had a better than average day on 30 July when 25 to 30 Bf109s, soon joined by an additional eight to 12 Messerschmitts and Mc202s, made the mistake of trying to dogfight 36 Warhawks from the 317th and 319th FSs near Alghero in southern Sardinia. As a result 21 Bf109s were claimed destroyed and three probably destroyed for the loss of Lt Bob Sederberg who was shot down and taken prisoner.

The Checkertails provide us with an interesting statistic since they flew in turn P-40 Warhawks, P-47 Thunderbolts and P-51 Mustangs in Africa and Italy. While destroying a total of 534 enemy aircraft in aerial combat, their kill-loss ratios were 3.6 : 1 in Warhawks, 3.9 : 1 in Thunderbolts and 3.2 : 1 flying Mustangs (figures from *Checkertail Clan*).

The desert war was highly significant because it established the principles upon which the proper use of air power was based from that time onwards. The one man most responsible for proving these concepts was Air Chief Marshal Arthur Tedder (he was of course supported by his boss, Gen Alexander, and many like-minded air officers, including Gen Tooey Spaatz), and chief among the tools Tedder possessed were the Tomahawk, Warhawk and Kittyhawk.

The Warhawks and Kittyhawks were employed in Italy exactly as Tedder had demonstrated that they should be; and it is bootless to hold that any other 'bomb-carrying fighter' could have performed better, because these were the aircraft that were there when needed, and their pilots did the job, and did it very well indeed.

Below: **An RAF No 260 Squadron Kitty is salvaged from the desert near El Assa; February 1943.**/*Frank F. Smith*

Left: **It is unlikely that the rudder art on this 325th FG Warhawk survived after the group commander discovered it. Perhaps the pilot hoped it would impede the aim of any Messerschmitt pilot that chanced to get on his tail.**

Above left: **Merlin-powered Kittyhawk Mk IIs, lightweight versions of the P-40F, flown by RAAF No 3 Squadron. This photo probably taken during the Sicilian campaign.** /*Frank F. Smith*

Left: **Kittyhawk Mk IVs (P-40N) of RAAF No 450 Squadron at Vasto, Italy late in 1943. The Aussies were also pretty good combat artists.**/*Frank F. Smith*

Above: **Show biz personalities visit the 57th FG in Tunisia. Frances Langford and Bob Hope are flanked (left to right) by Lt Don McGoldrick (!), CO Robert L. Baseler and Lt Wallace Kotter.**/*US Army*

Right: **In the western desert 'maintenance' facilities were approximately equal for men and machines; 57th FG.**/*Archie Knight*

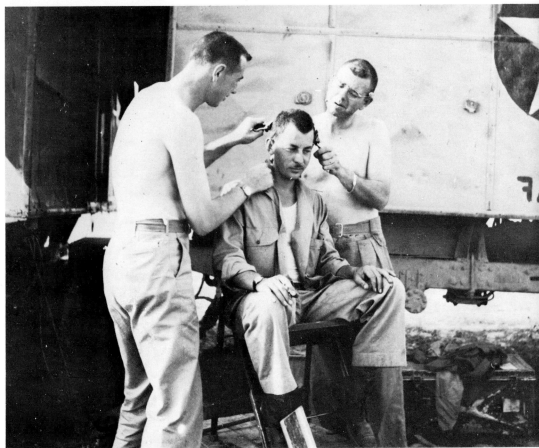

69

Right: **Capt Charles B. Hall shot down two Bf109s and an Fw190 over Sicily and Italy; is today an FAA official at the FAA Aeronautical Centre in Oklahoma City.**/*USAF*

Far right: **Col Benjamin O. Davis Jr, first CO of the 99th FS; later CO of the all-Negro 332nd FG, and eventually, as Lt-Gen Davis, Commander of the 13th Air Force.**/*USAF*

Above: **Fuelling by hand from five-gallon tins was not unusual when the Kittys took over captured enemy aerodromes close upon the heels of advancing Allied troops.**
/*Frank F. Smith via Ernie McDowell*

Right: **SAAF No 4 Squadron gave up its Kittyhawks to fly Spitfires in August 1943 while at Houaouria Landing Ground. The squadron had 105 aerial victories to its credit at the end of the African Campaign.**
/*Frank F. Smith via Ernie McDowell*

5 The China-Burma -India Theatre

Throughout World War II the exploits of fighter pilots in China, Burma and India (CBI) received the attention of publicists and reporters on a regular basis. The pilots actually doing the flying could not have cared less – they were in 'shoe-string outfits, always outnumbered, under-supplied and inadequately supported. It was a frontier air force, living at the end of the longest supply line of the war, more comparable to our western cavalry outposts of the late 1800s than to any 20th century military unit', according to former 23rd Fighter Group commander and AVG observer Bruce K. Holloway.

Two factors combined to ensure a 'romantic' picture of the CBI: the American Volunteer Group (AVG or Flying Tigers) and the Curtiss Hawk 81, forever the P-40 to the American public. In the terrible first weeks of December 1941, America was suffering daily at the hands of the conquering Japanese . . . with one exception. The Flying Tigers took their P-40s into action after Pearl Harbor and from 20 December onwards outfought their Japanese counterparts. The dejected American public ate up their exploits and the P-40 forever became a favourite fighter plane in the US as did the 'romantic' CBI.

That so much morale boosting and effective combat flying was being done this early in the Pacific war had nothing to do with American foresight – the facts tell the oppo-. site. Through more than five years of frustrating roadblocks, retired Army Air Corps Captain Claire Lee Chennault worked at building an air force for the Nationalist Chinese.

Chennault had been an original thinker in pursuit aviation in an era of the 'invincibility' of the heavy bomber. He believed that a well led force of fighters could stop a large force of bombers. This was not a popular position in the Air Corps of the 1930s and he left in the spring of 1937, 47 years old and suffering from slight deafness. By summer he was in China with an undertrained and under equipped air force to face a full scale invasion by Japan. By October 1937 the Nationalist Chinese Air Force had but a few Curtiss Hawk IIIs left. Even with the help of the Soviet Union, China was not able to rebuild its air force into an effective tool.

By August 1940 Soviet help diminished and the Japanese introduced to combat their A6M2 Zero-Sen fighter. The situation was hopeless. Chennault, by early 1941, was back in the US with Gen Pan Tsu Mow with a bold new plan – obtain modern American aircraft flown by American pilots to fight the Japanese. That Chennault ever realised even a limited measure of his dream is amazing.

Madam Chiang Kai-shek, the National Secretary of Aviation and, some have said, the real power in Nationalist China, had given Chennault $8,900,000 under a proper private corporation, China Defense Supplies, chartered by the State of Delaware, to get what was needed. Chennault outlined the situation in China to Burdette Wright, and said confidently that he would seriously impede the Japanese march through south-east Asia and that Madam Chiang would therefore reconsider her threat to negotiate with the Japanese – if Chennault had a group each of fighters and bombers properly manned.

Along with Curtiss-Wright 'export representative' William D. Pawley, Chennault was assured delivery of the Tomahawk fighters he wanted. One hundred H81-A2s earmarked for the RAF were billed to China by C-W beginning 6 January 1941, some time before Chennault arrived in the US, indicating prior agreement for purchase.

Chennault, no doubt aided by Pawley's collected friends in high places, held discussions with Navy Secretary Frank Knox, Treasury secretary Henry Morgenthau, Jr and presidential adviser Thomas Corcoran about forming an 'American Volunteer Group' in China. On 15 April 1941 President Roosevelt signed an executive order, without publicity, authorising the recruitment of reserve military personnel for the AVG through the Central Aircraft Manufacturing Company, Pawley's Burma-based company.

Recruiting was underway immediately at USAAC and USN bases. A one year contract was required of each recruit, with pay ranging

Top: **The Hawk 81-A2 of Charles H. 'Chuck' Older, 'Hell's Angels' (3rd) Squadron of the American Volunteer Group. The four .30cal wing guns and the two .50s in the nose packed a good wallop. Older, a former Marine pilot, claimed 10¼ kills with the Flying Tigers and later came back as a Lt-Col in the 14th Air Force to finish the war as the 14th's leading ace with 22½.**
/Tom Haywood

Above: **R. T. Smith claimed 8⅔ victories with the AVG. Smith thought the P-40 was reliable, could take a real beating and still get back home—if pointed in the right direction, the fighter, he thought and proved, could get pretty good results.**
/R. T. Smith

from $250 to $750 per month, plus travel expenses, 30 days annual leave with pay, free quarters, a valet/interpreter and $30 per month for rations. Top pay of $750 went to squadron leaders, pilots receiving $600. Not included in the contracts was the promise of a $500 bonus from the Chinese government for each Japanese plane shot down. The contracts were to 'manufacture, repair and operate aircraft', covering anything Chennault wanted to do.

Pawley, along with his chief recruiter, Richard Aldworth, did a remarkable job in going after the authorised 350 men. Pilots came from both pursuit and bombardment groups of the USAAC. Bell and Consolidated lost test pilots. The USS *Saratoga* lost three men to the AVG, the USS *Wasp* contributed one. Five Navy PBY pilots left the world of straight and level to become Tigers. Commercial pilots joined as well. In all, about half of the recruited pilots were Marine or Navy

pilots, about one third came from the USAAC and the rest were commercial or test pilots.

By mid-May 1941 the crated Hawk 81-A2s began to find their way to Rangoon Harbour, along with Allison engine specialist Walter E. Pentecost who had been recruited from North American Aviation. On 7 July the first contingent of AVG personnel – 110 pilots, 150 mechanics and a few support men – sailed from San Francisco posing as bankers, actors, clergymen and even circus entertainers. Via Singapore, they arrived at Toungoo, a primitive former RAF airstrip, on the 28th. Kunming, the AVG's intended base, was not ready and the temporary base had but one redeeming feature amidst the poor facilities – a 4,000ft asphalt runway.

The Hawks were assembled at Mingaladon airfield near Rangoon under Pentecost's supervision and tested between 1 August and 1 December, being delivered to Kyedaw. Though much of the assembly was through raw manpower, construction of the Hawks went very well. The Allison V-1710-C15 engines suffered from leaky front thrust bearings until Pentecost improvised a plate attached to the bottom of the thrust bearing plate to act as a sump. Faulty ammunition was also a problem for months and replacement parts were nonexistant.

Chennault arrived on 22 August to find his 'CAMCO employees' suffering heat, bad food and mosquitos in grass huts. He wasted no time in teaching his theories of fighter combat using the P-40, as the H81-A2s were always known in the AVG. At least half the pilots had never seen a P-40 and training was slow – three pilots died in training accidents, others quit and went home while the Old Man talked about exploiting the P-40s speed and diving ability to deny the Japanese superiority in climb and manoeuvrability. Torrential rain and minor accidents kept the Hawks on the ground a great deal.

C. H. 'Link' Laughlin, one of the USMC pilots to join the AVG, had his own version of what it was like:

'The AVGs were, for the most part, Navy trained. Approximately 50 Navy and Marine pilots – about 35 Army Air Corps, flying the P-40, an Air Corps product.

'Navy flight training stresses the carrier approach. Got to be tail first to get the hook into the arresting cable. And a full stall landing. So, it's a nose high, hang-it-on-the-prop approach attitude. Then full stall, tail down, and CRASH on the deck. The approved method.

'It was the basis of the chipped-tooth syndrome among Navy pilots who had to learn to land with teeth clenched.

'Navy aircraft are so designed with short, stubby engines – radial – so the pilot can see the deck and the landing signal officer. The

P-40 with its long snout was positively not suitable for this methodology. The approved method was wheels first, an arduous problem for the Navy pilots. But they learned – after contributing a number of P-40s to the spare parts department.'

The training course was to consist of 60 hours familiarisation flying and mock combat, 72 hours of lectures. Pilots paired off for simulated combat as Chennault watched from the tower with a radio mike in his hand to 'lecture' those upstairs. The pilots had a rough time learning to wheel land the P-40, as Laughlin has pointed out. Many were overshooting the field and ground-looping at the other end, damaging the aircraft and wearing out brakes. Chennault finally ordered a white line painted one third the way down each runway. Anyone who overshot the line was fined $50. The problem disappeared in a short time.

The AVG's primary duty was to help protect Chiang Kai-shek's supply routes through Burma. Seventy Japanese Army squadrons with 620 aircraft (340 fighters) opposed the AVG from bases in China, Indo China and Thailand. By 1 December all Japanese Navy aircraft had been pulled out of China proper but 191 remained on Hainan (including 70 Zero-Sens) across the Gulf of Tonkin.

As things turned out, the AVG did not see action until after Pearl Harbor. When news of the Japanese assault reached Chennault, he moved his 'volunteers' to Kunming at the eastern end of the Burma Road. The field was unfinished in a mountain valley 6,000ft above sea level.

The group was divided into three squadrons of 18 planes each – at no time did the AVG possess more than 55 flyable fighters after going into combat. The First Pursuit Squadron was the 'Adam and Eve' to commemorate the first pursuit in history, led by Robert Sandell; the Second was the 'Panda Bears', Jack Newkirk leading; the Third called themselves 'Hell's Angels' with Arvid Olson leading.

Just before Pearl Harbor, several AVG pilots saw a magazine article illustrating RAF Squadron No 112 in the Western Desert with their shark mouthed Tomahawks – within weeks every Hawk in the AVG was so decorated. The term 'Flying Tigers' seems to have come from the 30 March 1942 issue of *Life* magazine – the AVG pilots liked this and picked up the title.

Erik Shilling, Allen Christman and Ed Rector flew the AVG's first mission on 10 December, a reconnaissance from Rangoon 400 miles to Bangkok to assess Japanese air strength – they found nearly 100 enemy aircraft within easy striking distance of Rangoon. Chennault split his group, sending the Third to Mingaladon to fight with RAF No 67 Squadron, which flew antiquated Brewster Buffaloes.

First combat came on 20 December as warning came of 10 Ki21 Sally bombers approaching from Indo-China. The Chinese early warning network was active with great effectiveness – Chennault's observers, all Chinese, surrounded Kunming 62 miles, 125 miles and 185 miles out, listening for enemy aircraft. When an enemy formation approached, they were to pick up telephones and relay the information on. Throughout the war this 'Jing Bao' system worked.

When the enemy formation was about 60 miles out, Newkirk led Christman, Rector and Bright to intercept the bombers while four more Panda Bears followed to fly top cover. Sixteen Adam and Eve Hawks then flew to an auxiliary field south-east of Kunming.

Below: **The Chinese were master craftsmen with bamboo and paper. The AVG put this to good use, as can be seen here at Kunming, and several were blazed to bits by raiding enemy aircraft.**

Newkirk's flight found the Sallys about 30 miles south-east of Kunming and Ed Rector got one on his first pass. Then the AVG's oldest pilot, 43-year old Louis Hoffman (an ex-Navy chief) got one just before Sandell's Adam and Eves arrived. Fritz Wolfe added two more to the victory list. The unescorted enemy bombers were jettisoning their bombs and turning for home as all the fireworks took place, not expecting such ferocity from Chennault's small force. No Hawks were lost but Ed Rector ran out of gas and bellied into a rice paddy.

Chennault gave a few words of praise, several more of criticism, then added, 'Next time, get them all'. Later reports came in that three more of the Ki21s had failed to return to base.

On 23 December 48 Sallys of the 7th and 10th Air Groups, escorted by 20 Ki27 and Ki43 fighters (Nates and Oscars), came across the Gulf of Martaban for Rangoon. Olson's Hell's Angels scrambled 12 P-40s along with the Buffaloes of No 67 Squadron only to miss the first wave but they tangled with the remaining 30 bombers and their fighter escort. Ken Jernstedt and Charles Older exploded a bomber – the falling debris collided with Neil Martin's Hawk and a Japanese gunner shot down Hank Gilbert. A pair of enemy fighters shot up Paul Greene's P-40, forcing him to bail out.

Older flamed another bomber and other Tigers claimed three more bombers and four fighters. Chennault considered the trade a bad one – there were too few P-40s and pilots to go around if the AVG was going to give the Japanese a long term threat.

Link Laughlin, like most of the others, made it through his first encounter by sheer confusion:

'One minute I was tooling along after my flight leader attending to my wing man duties – and the next minute my flight leader disappears in some odd ball manoeuvre I've got yet to figure out. The neighbourhood proliferates with Zeros like flies in a garbage dump.

'I sense a problem. My cerebral apparatus goes into high gear and develops a number of short circuits. One set of neurons signal, "Go RIGHT!" Another group holler, "LEFT ...left...le...!" And still others scream, "ACTION ... ANYTHING ..." So, what happens? I breeze through the swarm with crossed controls. The Japs have never seen a P-40 flying sideways. A helluva tough target to hit. I credit my survival to this innovative manoeuvre hitherto never recommended by the experts.'

Laughlin finished an AVG ace with 5.2 victories.

On Christmas Day, the 12 flyable Hell's Angels and 18 RAF Buffaloes met 71 enemy Ki21s with an escort of 30 to 40 Ki43s and Ki27s. The Tigers had learned their lesson well three days earlier and methodically cut through the formation in pairs, the wingmen keeping track of the fighters as the leaders went after the bombers. Duke Hedman claimed two bombers and three fighters; George McMillan claimed two more; Chuck Older got four and Tadpole Smith claimed three in spite of one of his .50cal guns firing out of control. Jernstedt added another to his score and Parker DuPuoy closed in so tight one wing of his Hawk almost cut an enemy fighter in half. The Nate tumbled down out of control and DuPuoy flew home minus four feet of wing.

That day 32 enemy aircraft were claimed for the loss of two Hawks and *no* pilots – seven of the claims were made by the Buffalo pilots. The AVG had produced three aces (Smith, Older and Hedman) that day in the

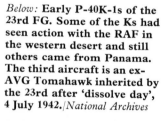

Below: **Early P-40K-1s of the 23rd FG. Some of the Ks had seen action with the RAF in the western desert and still others came from Panama. The third aircraft is an ex-AVG Tomahawk inherited by the 23rd after 'dissolve day', 4 July 1942.**/*National Archives*

process, setting a record for claims in one day they would not better.

The Japanese were in earnest at the Allied reaction they had caused, admitting, for the first time, heavy losses. Action continued around Rangoon so Chennault sent 'Scarsdale Jack' Newkirk's Panda Bears to relieve the Hell's Angels. In the first 10 weeks, the Tigers encountered the enemy 31 times over Burma, claimed 217 enemy aircraft and listed another 43 probables for the loss of 16 Hawks and six pilots. The Adam and Eves were rotated to Mingaladon to share in the fighting as well, and the RAF replaced its tattered Buffaloes with Hurricanes.

On 15 February 1942, Singapore fell and 85,000 British troops surrendered to the Japanese – the enemy advance was evident everywhere and Allied units, including the

AVG were forced to evacuate and fight more than once. When the Tigers arrived at Magwe about 20 flyable P-40s were left. Chennault, most likely through 10th Air Force commander Gen Lewis Brereton, managed to wangle several new P-40Es into the AVG in March and April, bringing total strength in mid-April to 36 combat-worthy aircraft and 39 under repair. Of the latter, 22 were destroyed by the Tigers themselves when they were forced to abandon Loiwing on 1 May.

By then the morale of the Tigers was sinking amidst the resignations or 'dishonourable discharges', as Chennault preferred to call them, of several pilots and ground crew. Often the pilots found themselves flying numerous low-level 'morale raising' missions ordered by Chiang. Three P-40s would over-fly Chinese ground positions to prove that

Left: **Left to right: Lt-Gen Henry H. 'Hap' Arnold, Chief, USAAF; Brig-Gen Claire Lee Chennault, 14th Air Force; Lt-Gen Joseph W. Stilwell; Sir John Dill; and Brig-Gen Clayton L. Bissell meeting at the start of the 1943 limited offensive. Chennault and Bissell were at continued odds in supplying the China Air Task Force, then the 14th Air Force.**/*USAF*

Below: **Chinese and American pilots of the Chinese-American Composite Wing working up on the P-40 in India. The CACW was formed of American trained Chinese pilots with American instructors for the purpose of supplying the Chinese Air Force with national air power. Left to right: Lt Chang SS, Lt Loyd B. Yost, Lt Ku Po and Lt W. W. Walton.**/*USAF*

Above: **A captured A6M2 Zero-Sen in Chinese Nationalist markings (even a tail number similar to the AVG Hawks) at Kunming with a 23rd FG P-40 in February 1943. Pilots testing the aircraft were impressed with both its sterling flying characteristics and its excessive vulnerability.** */USAF*

friendly air support existed. In the smoke, haze and with several bounces by Japanese fighters, the missions were very unpopular, not to mention frequent enemy flak when the Tigers wandered over the ever changing lines of battle.

On 23 April the pilots of the 2nd and 3rd Squadrons confronted Chennault and refused to fly any more 'morale raising' missions or fly escort for the terribly slow RAF bombers. Twenty-three pilots resigned before the crisis was averted through Madam Chiang's intervention. Individualists to the last, the Flying Tigers were forever chafing at being treated like military personnel when their contracts specified them to be civilians hired to fight for China. Regardless, they fought on in what many have called the most effective groups of fighter pilots ever formed. On 4 July 1942, 'Dissolve Day', the Tigers were to be inducted into the USAAF as the 23rd FG, a part of Chennault's China Air Task Force.

Only five pilots and 17 mechanics chose to be inducted in the Army Air Force out of 87 pilots and 164 ground support personnel. Fifty-five did volunteer for an extra two weeks to help the inexperienced Army pilots but the Tigers remained true to their civilian status for the most part.

During the 30 weeks the American Volunteer Group flew combat, it claimed 297 confirmed destroyed, up to 240 unconfirmed destroyed in the air, and 40 destroyed on the ground. Four Tigers were lost in air combat, six died from ground fire while strafing, three were lost in training accidents, three to enemy bombing and three were taken prisoner by the Japanese. Twelve Hawks were

destroyed in aerial combat and another 61 were written off in training accidents, were destroyed on the ground by the enemy or were set afire by the AVG upon evacuating Loiwing. Twenty-six aces emerged from the ranks of the Tigers – two later earned the Medal of Honor (Pappy Boyington and Jim Howard).

Chennault agreed to accept induction of the AVG into the USAAF since he was promised higher priority in obtaining supplies and much needed equipment. On 9 April 1942 he was promoted to the rank of colonel and six days later to brigadier-general under the assumption that the AVG would form the nucleus of the new CATF. Unfortunately friction between Clayton Bissel (one of Gen Joe Stilwell's aides who was promoted to brig-gen one day before Chennault) and Chennault led to threats of draft against the AVG personnel if they did not accept induction into the Army.

The USAAF earmarked the AVG to become the 23rd FG on 4 July but few of the experienced heads stayed, although several came back into the US armed services later. On 3 July Chennault received a pitiful response to the promises of more equipment – 16 P-40Es and 22 pilots of the 16th FS. With the 28 Hawk 81-A2s (18 serviceable) and 18 P-40Es of the AVG, Chennault had 51 airworthy fighters and 24 veteran pilots. Ten P-43s were thrown in by the Chinese, which did not help any since they were flying fire bombs.

The AVG volunteers were split up between the 75th Squadron at Kweilin, the 76th at Hengyang and the 74th (used as the nursery

squadron for the least combat-ready USAAF pilots) at Kunming. For the first two weeks the 23rd was commanded by one of the extra-time volunteers, Bob Neale, still considered a civilian by the Army.

Regardless of their unfulfilled contracts (no 30 days leave with pay or a trip home), the volunteers flew combat, losing two (one killed, one missing) of their number. On 18 July replacement Army pilots arrived and the last of the Flying Tigers, with the exception of the five pilots who decided to become part of the USAAF, went home.

Chennault's CATF began operations with quite a reputation to follow. A handful of B-25s were added to his force under Col Caleb V. Haynes but replacements never did pour in. Even though the CATF became the 14th Air Force in early 1943, total strength of the 14th never exceeded about 500 fighters

Right: **Lt Don Taylor, newly arrived at the 51st FG, January 1943, after patrol duty with the 51st FS in Panama. Ah, those gaberdine flight suits were nice—at altitude!** /*Don Taylor*

Far right: **A captured 'Oscar-type Zero' at Kweilin. Every single engine fighter the Japanese operated in the CBI was known as a Zero for some time, regardless of its actual type.**/*Don Lopez*

Bottom right: **The 51st FG's 'B-40s' line up for a dive bombing mission with 1,000lb bombs. The bombs were not listed as capable of being carried by the P-40 but John Barr, Group CO, thought these medium bomber eggs would be great for busting bridges and railroad tracks—he was right.**/*USAF*

and 175 bombers. In the summer of 1942 this force was to cover an area roughly the size of western Europe and one year later the P-40 force had but 64 operational fighters.

The reason for this austerity was not just low priority on equipment. The 14th operated at the end of the longest and most difficult supply line of World War II. On an average it took from four to six months for a shipment from the US to reach Kunming. Everything was dependent on airlift over the Hump and transportation priorities frequently went to support for the Chinese ground forces. According to Bruce Holloway:

'At times even oxcarts had priority over gasoline and ammunition for the small 14th Air Force.

'For a period of two to three months, the 75th FS at Ling Ling had nothing but five gallon cans with which to refuel their aircraft, no cars or trucks, not even a typewriter. Ammunition boxes were carried on the backs of coolies. There was just one radio, and it could reach Kunming, about 600 miles away, only between the hours of 1700 and 1830 in the evening. There was a certain advantage to this. Reports were written as briefly as possible in longhand, and I would wait until near the end of the transmission period to send my plan of action back to Gen Chennault at Kunming. The only way he could change it would be to send someone over by plane, since all communications stopped after dark.'

The first commander of the 23rd FG was Col Robert L. Scott, an adventurer if there ever was one. Arriving in China in April, he wangled a P-40 from Chennault and actually flew combat with the AVG. From May 1942 Bruce Holloway did the same as an 'observer'. Scott led the group until January 1943 when Holloway took over through the following September. The first squadron COs were inducted AVG veterans – Frank Schiel, Tex Hill and Ed Rector for the 74th, 75th and 76th respectively. The 16th Squadron of the 51st FG was also attached to the 23rd.

When the 14th became an entity in itself, separate from the 10th Air Force, only five groups were earmarked to fly the P-40, the CBI's main fighter – the 8th Photo Reconnaissance (10th AF, India), the 23rd Fighter (14th AF, China), the 33rd Fighter (12th, 10th and 14th AFs), the 51st Fighter (10th and 14th AFs), and the 80th Fighter (10th AF).

It took a while to get these groups up to par but before long top notch pilots emerged from the Stateside arrivals, among them John Alison and Albert 'Ajax' Baumler, and combat operations continued with as much vigour as possible. The 23rd was, at first, the only fighter group to oppose the Japanese in China but the enemy was not that active.

The 23rd followed what became a consistent course of air operations – bomb and strafe enemy airfields, troop and supply installations, prevent effective bombing by the Japanese air force.

Alison, Baumler, Tex Hill and E. W. Richardson quickly undertook the latter at 0200 hours, 30 July, when Japanese bombers attacked in strength during a moonlit night. The previous evening the enemy force had knocked out the stick and paper decoys around the perimeter at Hengyang and the 23rd pilots did not want them to get away with the real thing.

Without lights, the four P-40s lost visual contact with each other after take-off. Alison found three bombers at 15,000ft and attacked but his Hawk was riddled with 7.7mm fire. He continued the attack, sawing the wing off one Betty, then half rolled into a split-S. His engine caught fire as he dived for the safety of the field but another bomber got in the way – just as he flamed it, his engine quit.

Johnny came across Hengyang high, fast and burning. Too late to save the P-40, he ditched it in the Siang Rover. Baumler in another of the P-40 'Night Fighters' downed two bombers. Alison got the DSC for his effort.

The four squadrons of the CATF gradually received 'new' P-40Ks that had seen combat over the western desert with the RAF and patrol duty over Panama. At one point the CATF's P-40s were grounded for 33 days due to the lack of fuel.

One of the pilots who left for China from Panama was Don Taylor, who flew P-40Bs and Cs on patrol with the 51st FS from France Field, where he learned 'you never fly at night in a P-40 and you never fly instruments in a P-40'. Arriving in India to fly with the 51st FG out of Assam, he quickly learned to drop 500lb and 1,000lb bombs from the 'B-40'. As with all fighters in the CBI, most of the missions were strafing, bombing standing alert and flying patrol. Things were often very slow due to days and days of pouring rain.

Taylor remembers the great day he received a P-40E-1 with K wings, landing gear and tail. On his first flight the gear had to be pumped down and the engine quit twice in three days. Great fun, the CBI. A good P-40 pilot could make a tight tactical approach before the gear was down and locked by first putting the gear lever down, and then swapping hands and pumping the hydraulic pump. This took 20 seconds and some guys were down before the gear locked.

The Japanese would attack the 51st's field only every four or five months and Taylor never shot at an enemy plane in the air. Most losses were from dive bombing and strafing. The biggest raid he recalls was four B-24s

Above: **Vernon A. 'Sack' Tanner with his shot up P-40K, 75th FS, at Hengyang on 17 May 1944. Tanner and six other P-40s intercepted an incoming formation of Japanese fighters in sight of those at the field, to allow a flight of eight P-40s low on fuel to land. The seven Hawks made repeated passes through the 40 'Zeros', driving them off, but Tanner had to belly in with a shot up electrical system, tail, wings and cockpit.**/*Don Lopez*

Right: **On 5 July 1944 eight 75th FS P-40s escorted 12 B-25s north of Changsha. Near Hengyang 12 Oscars were spotted and a fight developed. Don Lopez shot one down and damaged another. Seeing a chute going down, he flew over for a look and was hit by terrible fire from an enemy he never saw —an explosive shell hit the armour behind his head with a horrendous bang and his left aileron was blown apart. A rolling dive to the right shook the Japanese pilot. When he got home, his crew chief couldn't believe it and Tex Hill admonished Lopez not to buck for a Purple Heart. Here Lopez (left) and Dick Jones look at the damage.**/*Don Lopez*

and 18 P-40s. There was also escort for the transports over the Hump.

Most of the 'B-40' dive bombing with 1,000lb bombs (in disregard of the tech orders) was done in northern Burma to hit single track railway bridges. The idea was cooked up by 51st Executive Officer John E. Barr when he got a good look at the 1,000lb bombs sent to his field in March 1943 for the medium bombers. The next day he got off with one of the bombs hung on his P-40's belly and knocked out the bridge south of Mogaung. From that point on it was SOP to use the big bombs – the Naga headhunters referred to the 'B-40s' as 'the double aeroplane which drops half'.

Everyone loved to fly the P-40 with the canopy open but Taylor said one had to make sure there was nothing loose behind the pilot or it would get sucked out on take-off. If the oil cap was off, oil would siphon out of the tank and onto the pilot!

By autumn 1943 the 80th FG was operating with the 51st as the Burma Banshees, wearing very distinctive skulls on the noses of their Hawks.

Before Bob Scott left for the States he assumed the leadership of Fighter Command, CATF in February 1943 and left some hints on the use of the P-40 in China. The 'obsolete' bird had consistently beat the best Japanese fighters, which were superior in climb and manoeuvrability, due to:
'1. Greater Strength – the P-40 is the strongest fighter plane I've ever flown . . . it will stand all the pilot can.
2. Diving Speed – due to clean lines and weight, P-40s are among the fastest diving ships in the world today.
3. Firepower – equipped with six .50cal machine guns, our P-40s' firepower is far

greater than that of the present Jap fighters. American pilots are superior in aerial gunnery. I think this is because many of you are game hunters.

4. American Leadership and Pilot Ability – due to their commander's knowledge both of Japanese psychology and the shortcomings of the Jap fighter planes, American pilots of both the AVG and the China Air Task Force have been able to so bring about their meetings with the enemy, that the P-40's superior strength, diving speed and firepower, have brought astounding results, which are several times to one in our favour.'

Improvisation had much to do with the success of the P-40 in China. Holloway thinks:

'We developed the first bad weather landing system in China, and probably the only one in which the ground equipment was a human ear rather than electronic gadgets. At Kunming we had a let-down pattern worked out very similar to those used by jet aircraft today. The real trick was establishing the initial point and heading. This was done by a radio operator on the ground listening for the engine noise and providing verbal steers until we were on an approximately correct

Below: **The 80th FG's P-40Ns warm up for an escort mission to Burma, February 1944, just before painting their Hawks with the well known skull motif.** /*USAF*

Bottom: **The P-40N of 80th FG CO Col Ivan W. McElroy with a 500lb Christmas present for Tojo, Nagahuli, Upper Assam, India in early 1944.**/*USAF*

heading. From there on we simply flew a teardrop pattern as we let down to land. While I was there, nobody ran into the ground.'

There was continual amazement among the pilots over the lack of Japanese effort to get rid of the 14th Air Force. After the war General Takahashi, Chief of Staff of the Japanese armies in North China said, 'But for the 14th Air Force, we could have gone anywhere we wished in China'. Bruce Holloway again comments:

'It must surely have been known to them that at Kunming, the eastern terminus of the Hump run, there was rarely more than three or four days supply of fuel and ammunition for the Air Force units which protected the terminus area.

'If the Japanese had been willing to expend the effort for a few days running, the defences would have folded and Kunming could probably have been taken by a relatively modest airborne force. This would have been the end of our air operations in China.'

During the summer of 1943, the Chinese-American Composite Wing was formed on two groups, the 3rd and 5th, each with four squadrons, mostly equipped with P-40Ks. The Japanese Army squadrons were in the process of re-equipping with Ki43 Oscar IIs and the Ki44 Tojo. The Navy Zero-Sen then in service in the CBI was primarily the A6M3 Model 32.

By mid-June 1943, the 14th Air Force at last went on a consistent offensive under Brig-Gen Casey Vincent, the youngest US general officer since Custer. Casey took three squadrons of the 23rd Group to Kweilin along with 15 B-25s of the 11th Bombardment Group to attack the Japanese in East China. By 26 August they had claimed 91 destroyed and 26 probables for a loss of 26 Hawks.

Through mid-1944 Japanese positions in China remained static for the most part except for a thrust westward toward India's Assam valley and a southward thrust from the Tung Ting lake area. Their air power had dwindled significantly, due in large part to the 23rd's tenacity in using their P-40s.

Don Lopez was one of the replacement P-40 pilots to enter the theatre via the Fighter Training Replacement Unit at Landhi, near Karachi. When he arrived at Kweilin in November 1943, 23rd CO Tex Hill was sitting in a bare office with an IN basket full of peanuts and an OUT basket full of shells – that was all that there was on his bare desk. Lopez started to salute but Tex quickly grabbed his hand and said it was great to have some new pilots. Hill placed Lopez in the 75th Squadron, 'the best . . . my old outfit', at Hengyang.

Below: **The 80th used revetments at Upper Assam that served as fine camouflage, February 1944.** /*USAF*

Right: **John C. 'Pappy' Herbst was one of the 'old men' in the CBI and he led the 74th FS with great skill after flying with the 76th. His P-40 was named after his son (Pappy was divorced) and here he stands in the centre flanked by his Executive Officer, Ted Adams (left), and his Ops Officer, Charlie 'Smokey' Cook. Herbst finished the war with 20 victories.**
/Charlie Cook

Below: **The very distinctive 23rd FG base at Kweilin. The field was very easy to spot from a distance due to the many pointed hills.**
/Charlie Cook

Lopez flew several strafing missions to begin with, taking part in his first Jing Bao or scramble on 12 December. After jettisoning tanks when the bombers were spotted, the P-40s waded into the middle of 35 to 40 Oscars in 'squirrel cage' formation. Lopez didn't know what was going on, getting separated in the confusion. He spotted an Oscar chasing a P-40, got closer and squirted off a burst to get the Japanese pilot's attention ... the Oscar turned around head on for Lopez. Both pilots were getting strikes and Lopez fully expected the enemy pilot to turn first. At the last moment the Oscar whipped right, catching its left wing on the P-40's left wing. The Japanese fighter's wing ripped out at the root and three feet of Lopez's

wing disappeared. The Oscar went in; Lopez found another Oscar and two P-40s so continued to fight. The Hawk did not fly any differently with part of a wing gone!

Lopez helped the other two P-40s surround the Oscar, even though his Hawk was out of ammunition and shredded quite a bit. The Oscar was downed. Lopez recalls, 'I wasn't smart enough to worry about it and I just kept making passes at him. I truthfully didn't notice any major difference in the flying characteristics.'

Lost, he joined up with a flight of P-40s from the 26th Squadron. But they tried to join up on him, mistaking him for Bill Grosvenor, the Ops Officer – and they were on different frequencies! Lopez kept flying slower and slower so they'd get ahead – in a giant circle – until finding another Hawk, which turned out to be flown by Lopez's flight leader, who led them home. He did a classic double take as Lopez tucked in tighter than normal. 'We just peeled off and landed without giving it a second thought. If I'd known better I would have stalled it to see how it handled. Had to put a new wing on the aircraft. That was my first real combat experience with an aeroplane'.

One of the most effective weapons in use by the P-40 was the parafrag, carried on almost all the 23rd's bombing missions. With three on each wing, pilots dropped them all at once. Lopez remembers the chute on one catching on the wing of a P-40 and blowing the wing off.

The monsoon of 1943-44 kept operations scarce until the spring of 1944 but the 23rd began to work up on Mustangs. First the

P-51A and then the P-51B, allowing the group to range farther into enemy territory. Often mixed bags of P-51s and P-40s would fly together since the 23rd did not finish with their Hawks until late 1944.

As the Japanese pushed both from the south and from the north in May 1944 to cut China in half, the 23rd was forced to retreat from Hengyang to Ling Ling. The 75th Squadron returned to their old base and had the pleasure of bombing their former quarters, finally getting to kill the rats that had infested the place.

On 26 May the Mustangs and Hawks of the 23rd, flying out of Ling Ling, teamed up to fight several Oscars on the way back from the last strafing mission of the day. Balderson got lost in the weather and finally broke out over Chamsha, out of gas. Attempting to belly into Yale Street, he was severely injured. The 75th Flight Surgeon, J. D. 'Doc' Laughlin, parachuted out of a C-47 to render aid but the pilot was dead by the time Doc arrived.

The new P-40N began to arrive and the pilots were very pleased with it since it was the lightest of the Hawks. Don Lopez picked one up and flew it to Calcutta for a food run. Meals in China were consistently horrible and everyone suffered from the GIs. It was unheard of to ferry an empty aircraft back from India where the excellent commissary stocked quite a selection. Lopez bought three barracks' bags full of food and crammed them into the P-40 from the tail wheel forward by crawling into the fuselage – each bag was too heavy to lift so he was forced to unload each one into the fighter, along with his B-4 bag, a new phonograph and as many records as he could buy.

When he jumped into the cockpit, he could not move the stick! Too much food jammed against the control cables. After rearranging the goodies (heaven forbid he *leave* any of it behind), he fired up. As the aircraft gathered

speed, the tail never came up – the old N simply went straight up with full forward stick and full nose down trim. Fortunately the Allison was delivering enough power to make the out of balance fighter fly. Arriving at Moenbury, Lopez could not get the main gear on to the runway – the tail wheel hit and the P-40 sailed down the runway with the mains off until she stalled. 'Fighter pilots thought CG meant Commanding General,' recalled Lopez.

By December 1944 there were still 205 P-40s in the CBI but the P-51 and P-47 were in the forefront by then. Don Lopez converted to the P-51C along with the rest of the 75th Squadron and flew the rest of his combat tour in the Mustang, gaining a fifth kill before it was over. He preferred the P-40 over the P-51 for the type of combat in the CBI. The canted guns in the early Mustangs continually

Above: **The 23rd Group control cave at Kweilin. Here the famous ears-eyes-telephone warning net ended. Rarely were there any surprise attacks, so effective were the Chinese at detecting incoming formations.**/*Charlie Cook*

Below: **November 1944—a 23rd FG P-40N leaves the US Chinese Air Service Command operated factory at Kunming. The Hawk had been brought in unserviceable and was overhauled by Chinese and American mechanics.**
/*US Army*

jammed unless the pilot did not put any Gs on the aircraft, a great liability in air to air combat. The 23rd's experience was gained in the P-40 and it will remain the favourite. When counting the 297 kills of the AVG, the 23rd finished the highest scoring American Air Force group of the war with 1,238 confirmed destroyed – not bad considering that, throughout the war, China was always outside the main theatre of combat. These fighter pilots were always vastly outnumbered, isolated and at the bottom for resupply. Bruce Holloway thinks this 'bred a spirit of independence, daring and improvisation which was not equalled in any other theatre.'

Above: **Charlie 'Smokey' Cook's P-40N at Kweilin, May 1944. Note the newly arrived P-51Bs. Cook flew his P-40 with the 51s until late in the year and remembers flying through jettisoned parafrags in a dog-fight, flying 25 hours of combat in 72 hours and just being worn out.**/*Charlie Cook*

Left: **Robert 'Duke' Hedman's No 92 nosed up at Kunming. This 3rd Pursuit, 'Hell's Angels' Hawk with a red stripe around the fuselage appears to have had the Chinese National insignia painted over a blocked out RAF roundel.**/*Tom Haywood*

Right: Here is Charles Older's well known No 68 from the 3rd Pursuit. Chuck went on to gain a total of 10¼ victories with the Tigers. Note the patch above the eye on the nose—often panels were interchanged during maintenance and two eyes would result. /Tom Haywood

Below right: AVG ace Tom Haywood (centre) with two other Tigers at Mingaladon near Rangoon. The 'Hell's Angels' insignia took several forms but all were variations of a favourite theme./Tom Haywood

Below: 17 December 1944—three of the 205 P-40s left in the CBI. The Gooney Bird is landing here at Paoshan to pick up Chinese 8th Army troops. These 25th FS P-40Ns were a part of the 51st Group attached to the 14th Air Force and provided air cover for the transports. Seldom did they see action for the rest of the war as the P-51, P-47 and P-38 ranged far ahead to confront the enemy. /US Army

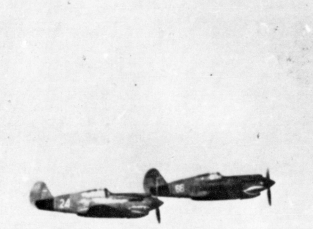

Above left: **A line up of 'Hell's Angels' Hawk 81s. Chennault was continually amazed the Japanese did not try to destroy the Flying Tigers on the ground since there was no protection or dispersal system to speak of. Lines of P-40s at Pearl Harbor suffered terribly.**

Left: **A formation of 'Hell's Angels' Hawks returning from a mission over Japanese occupied Burma. The rugged Yunnan mountains near the Chinese-Burmese border provide this March 1942 backdrop. Charles Older's No 68 leads the formation.**/*National Archives via Mike Minnich*

Above: **When the AVG's P-40Es were put into service in March 1942, they were not painted in individual squadron markings, carrying only the Bengal Tiger and sequential numbers picking up where the Hawk 81s left off, plus the ever present shark mouth.**/*via Ernest McDowell*

Below: **23rd FG P-40Ns in 1944, were in use as the P-51 began to replace them. Many pilots considered the P-40 better suited for combat in the CBI in spite of the Mustang's overall superiority.**/*Gary Frey via Ernest McDowell*

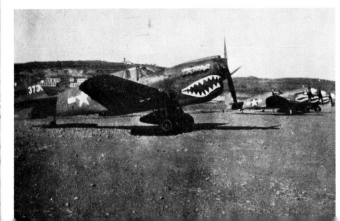

6 Aussies, Kiwis and Kittyhawks

The desert war in North Africa was only a foreshadowing of the extent to which the Australians would use their P-40s. The experience gained by the Aussies with their Hawk 81s (Tomahawks) was put to good use in both the Mediterranean and the Pacific when the first Hawk 87s (Kittyhawks) began to replace their older brothers.

As the first Kittys began to fly from the desert with Nos 3 and 450 Squadrons, Pearl Harbor changed priorities. The majority of Australia's air force was deeply involved in fighting the war in Europe and the Middle East. As hard as it was to believe, there was not a single fighter aircraft in the RAAF to protect their own continent.

The Japanese quickly attacked Malaya, Hawaii, Thailand, the Philippines, Guam, Wake Island and Hong Kong and by 22 January 1942 Rabaul fell. Three weeks later the first heavy raid on Darwin took place, then the Japanese turned towards Port Moresby in New Guinea. From here enemy forces could easily stage a major invasion of the Australian mainland. The Allies decided that Moresby would be held at all costs, despite the fact that seven Hudsons of No 32 Squadron and six Catalinas of No 11 Squadron constituted the entire strength of the RAAF in the area. No 24 Squadron's Wirraway 'fighters' had been decimated at Rabaul.

With a situation not unlike the proposed invasion of Britain by Germany a year and a half earlier, Australia could not hope to fare as well without sufficient fighters to oppose the waves of Japanese bombers that would do the softening up. At the end of February, 25 P-40Es were transferred from the USAAF to form the nucleus of RAAF No 75 Squadron at Townsville under Sqn Ldr Peter Jeffrey, a 12-victory fighter pilot who had commanded No 3 Squadron RAAF in the Middle East. During one of the ferry flights bad weather downed three aircraft and killed two pilots.

By 8 March Jeffrey began an intensive course in fighter tactics, gunnery and principles of fighter control that was finished just nine days later. On 19 March Flt Lt J. F. 'Old John' Jackson, another combat veteran

from No 3 Squadron was appointed CO and 17 Kittyhawks were flown off to Moresby by No 75's youngsters, most of whom had never seen an enemy aircraft. Staging by way of Cooktown and Horn Island, the first flight of four arrived over Seven Mile Drome on the 21st. After suffering 16 enemy air raids, the gunner's reactions were understandable – they opened fire on the Kittys! The barrage did not stop until Flt Lt P. Turnbull was on the ground and the other three Kittyhawks had lowered their landing gear. Three of the four were damaged, one so badly it was non-salvagable. Turnbull found a round buried in his headrest only an inch away from his head.

The other 16 fighters arrived an hour later but before they could get settled an alert was sounded. Flg Offs W. L. Wackett and B. M. Cox were scrambled to intercept a lone Sally making its routine daily recce of Moresby. Cox put the port engine out and Wackett placed a burst into the other, causing the bomber to lose altitude. At 500ft it exploded and crashed into the sea near the entrance to Port Moresby Harbour. Spirits at Moresby soared. For weeks the rumours had been flying about the arrival of the squadron and the aircraft had been dubbed 'Tomorrowhawks' and 'Neverhawks' in wry bull sessions.

The odds these green pilots faced were incredible. Out of No 75's entire roster of pilots, only three had ever flown a fighter in combat. The pilots of the Japanese Imperial Navy, on the other hand, were seasoned veterans who had obtained kills over China in the late 1930s. The superb fighter wing at Lae had such pilots as one of the highest scoring Japanese fighter pilots of the war, Lt Hiroyoshi Nishizawa, who ended his career with 103 victories, and Lt Saburo Sakai, a 64-kill ace.

The day after 75's arrival they were thrown into the desperate fight. At 0630 hours on 22 March nine Kittys took off to strafe Lae – reconnaissance had revealed 26 enemy aircraft on the field, including the new Betty bomber. After a diversion over the sea, the Hawks attacked out of surrounding cloud to sweep low over the enemy base – so low that the

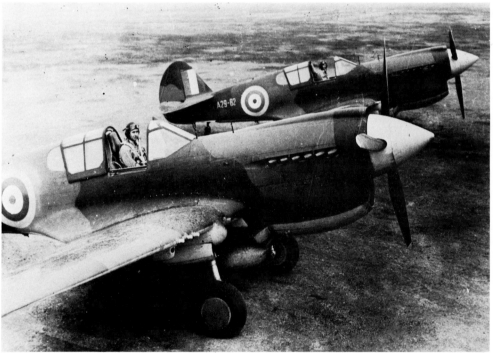

underside of Flt Lt J. W. W. Piper's Kitty struck one of the Japanese aircraft on the ground.

The enemy was completely surprised, causing Flt Lt Les Jackson, younger brother of the CO, to lead the flight back in for a second run. Twelve aircraft were left burning and another five were damaged.

The top cover of four P-40s encountered three Zeros flying standing patrol at 10,000ft.

Wackett evaded this formation and attacked another that had bounced the strafing force of five Kittys. As he made a beam attack, one of Wackett's guns failed. He broke away but his engine was hit in the process. Diving into cloud, he emerged to see two Zeros crash down into the sea, downed by Turnbull and Flt Lt J. H. S. Pettett.

Wackett's engine failed and he ditched 10 miles off shore between Lae and Salamaua.

Above: **No 75 Squadron RAAF, later joined by No 76, saw some of the heaviest fighting of the war at Port Moresby and Milne Bay in 1942. Here Flg Off Bruce Watson's *Stardust* (A29-136), a P-40E of No 75 Squadron, is seen at Milne Bay in 1942. The Japanese suffered their first major land defeat at Milne at the hands of the Australians and the victory is looked upon by many as the battle that saved Australia from invasion. Nos 75 and 76 squadrons were singled out as the decisive factor for their stopping of the Japanese forces the first day of the battle.**/*Frank F. Smith*

Left: **Even though the first RAAF Kittyhawk pilots did not go through formal operational training units, later OTUs were set up. Here two Kittys from No 2 OTU are seen at Mildura in June 1942, still carrying their original British camouflage and markings.**
/*H. Rodda via Frank Smith*

Above: **No 2 OTU gradually added markings to their P-40E Kittyhawks. These six are over Mildura, September 1942—three have an 'S' visible ahead of the national marking. The first four are serial numbers A29-119, A29-18, A29-82 and A29-91.**
|*H. Rodda via Frank Smith*

Right: **Here Flg Off Bruce Watson of No 75 Squadron stands with his *Stardust* at Cairns, Queensland in 1942. Note the absence of 'U' seen in the previous shot of the British national insignia. The photo was most likely taken before leaving for Port Moresby and action.**
|*Frank F. Smith*

Nine hours later, after evading sharks, he made it to shore without his boots. For four days he slogged through the jungle barefoot until reaching Bulwa and the New Guinea Volunteer Rifles. From there he made it back to Moresby, mostly on foot.

Flt Lt B. H. Anderson, seen turning to attack a Zero, caught several hits and went down, to be listed as MIA. In all the raid netted 14 destroyed for the loss of one pilot and two P-40s. A very good beginning that was soured the same day when three Kittyhawks were lost in a series of accidents.

The next day the Japanese retaliated with their 17th raid on Port Moresby. Around noon 19 bombers came in at high altitude and all the squadron's Kittys scrambled. Although the fighters were unable to intercept, the bombers did little damage. Four Zeros made

low level strafing runs and destroyed two Kittyhawks that had bogged down near the runway trying to get off. A third P-40 was damaged and one Zero was destroyed, another probably destroyed, by the airstrip's able gunners.

On 24 March Flt Lt John 'Hooley Dooley' Piper cornered a lone Japanese bomber south of Moresby and shot it down. Later in the day four P-40s intercepted 18 bombers approaching Moresby. Les Jackson waded into the three escorting Zeros and downed one in a head on attack. Anti-aircraft fire probably got one of the bombers.

The going was rough to say the least. In less than a week after their arrival, No 75 Squadron had lost 10 Kittys. With Jeffrey transferred to the mainland, 'Old John' Jackson was carrying the tremendous burden

Above: **Another P-40E from No 2 OTU, Mildura, Victoria, 1943. Serial number of the Kitty is A29-121.**
/Frank F. Smith

Left: **Sqn Ldr Stan Galton prepares to fire up his No 86 Squadron P-40M *Jen 1*, MP-A (A29-353) was Galton's mount in 1943-44 flying out of Merauke, Dutch New Guinea. Note the highly polished finish.**/*Frank F. Smith*

of the unit's battle out of Seven Mile. When not on strikes or operations, the pilots sat ready for scramble and they also kept a standing patrol in the air at all times. Warning of approaching enemy aircraft was often too late to get the P-40s to altitude and there was no fighter control for the sector. Living in a hard tropical climate without consistent food, these men had to face a lack of hard stands and an abundance of mud. One section of runway 400yds long was still being worked on, which made landings and take-offs a hazardous undertaking.

In spite of the struggle to mount an effective striking force, the squadron's reputation and morale were high. When North-Eastern Area HQ suggested No 75 Squadron return to Australia, Sqn Ldr Jackson, supported by Wg Cdr Pearce, RAAF Ops Officer at Moresby, protested strongly. The unit remained to fight and on 30 March the first five replacement aircraft arrived. One crashed and was seriously damaged.

During this time, No 75 Squadron was the only Allied fighter unit in the south-west Pacific Area opposing the Japanese in an offensive capacity since the other groups and squadrons of both the USAAF and RAAF were based in Australia. From the end of March, No 75 Squadron was giving and taking almost daily under the leadership of 34-year old Jackson, an 'old man' by the day's standards. On 10 April he was shot down by three Zeros as he was leaving Lae. Wading ashore, he walked out of the jungle in eight days. Five hundred natives cleared a strip at Wau and an American Dauntless, flown by Lt V. A. Schwab, came in covered

by Piper in a No 75 Squadron Kitty to pick Jackson up. As the two aircraft arrived over Seven Mile, three Zeros bounced them. Schwab evaded the attack and landed at an adjacent strip – Jackson never could get the rear gun to work and only after landing found the tip of his right index finger had been shot off.

By 28 April, Jackson could muster but five Kittyhawks for their last attack on Lae. On the way out they met a force of eight bombers with figher escort at 22,000ft headed for Moresby. In tight formation, the Hawks made a rear attack on the bombers as the lead Zero attacked Jackson, who spun out to avoid his foe, the other four Kitty pilots following suit.

In the ensuing fight, both Jackson and Cox were killed after getting a Zero. Flg Off J. Le Gay Brereton was severely wounded but he got his damaged Kitty back down. The CO's brother, Les, took command of No 75 Squadron the next day.

On 30 April No 75 was relieved of its air defence of Port Moresby. The pilots had flown 638 hours of combat in April alone and had but three serviceable and seven unserviceable fighters left. Since 21 March, 13 days after the Japanese had landed on the north coast of New Guinea, No 75 had been in the gap alone. The squadron's last sortie was flown on 3 May by Plt Off A. D. Tucker in the only serviceable Kitty when he took off with newly arrived American Airacobras to intercept 20 bombers and their fighter escort. The day before the other two Kittys had been written off (Sgt D. W. Munro was shot down and killed and one Kitty crashed on take-off).

In their 44 days at Port Moresby, No 75 Squadron pilots destroyed 35 enemy aircraft (18 in the air and 17 on the ground), got four probables and damged 47. Flt Lt Jackson shot four down with Piper and Masters getting $3\frac{1}{2}$ and two respectively. Twelve pilots and 22 Kittyhawks were lost, nine in known combat and four reported missing. Combat was so intense that each day's serviceability came to five on the average, and this was no reflection on the maintenance crews who worked around the clock to keep the Hawks airborne. But the mission had been accomplished – keep the Japanese at bay until 'more and better' could arrive.

When the 8th PG of the USAAF arrived with their P-400 Airacobras in late April to relieve No 75, it was with awe that the ground troops watched the squadron go. The Kitty pilots had been held in almost mystical reverence. Later the 35th FG arrived to help with more Airacobras. Never again would Australian pilots see such intense day to day combat, although much fighting remained ahead.

The Australians had yet to develop and produce a fighter for their own use. The Wirraway and later the Boomerang were built by the Commonwealth Aircraft Corporation but the RAAF needed fighters badly in 1942. It was clear the only immediate source would be the US with its lend lease policy. On 8 May 1942 711 Kittyhawks were ordered (the largest single aircraft order made by Australia) and the venerable P-40 became the RAAF's major aerial weapon of World War II, more Kittys being ordered up through 1944.

When the Japanese were denied Port Moresby by sea and air power, they decided to strike out over the Owen Stanley Mountains for this valuable city. Landing at Buna, the Japanese moved quickly to capture Milne Bay as well. Nos 75 and 76 Squadrons (the latter formed in April), re-equipped with Kittyhawks, arrived at No 1 Strip, Gurney, at the end of July amidst torrential rains and more mud gumbo. Sqn Ldr Leslie Jackson was still in command of No 75, the only survivor from the unit's original complement of pilots. Peter Turnbull was the CO of No 76 Squadron.

Although operations were started on 26 July, the first opportunity for aerial combat did not present itself until 4 August. No 76 Squadron had eight Kittyhawks on standing patrol when four Zeros and a Kate wandered into the Milne Bay area. The Zeros attacked Gurney and destroyed one of No 75's P-40s but Flt Lt P. H. Ash got the Kate. Sgts B. Carroll and P. Sempster shared a Zero while Flt Lt 'Bardy' Wawn claimed two Zeros as probables.

On the 11th another Japanese air raid was launched against Milne, only this time the newly operational radar station had given the Kitty pilots enough time to get to altitude and wait. Twenty-two Hawks met 12 Zeros but the inexperience of the Australians was paid for: three Zeros and one probable were claimed for the loss of four pilots. As much as the P-40 was deemed obsolescent by others, the Aussies considered it a first rate combat machine. This happened to be one of the rare times they came out behind in the give and take of aerial combat.

On the 24th a coast watcher reported the beginnings of an amphibious force of seven Japanese barges headed toward Milne Bay. The Kittyhawk squadrons were prevented from an early attack on the barges as 10 Zeros and two bombers attacked Gurney. Flt Lt V. Sullivan led eight No 76 Squadron fighters up followed by another 15 from No 75. The Australians got one of the Zeros and the anti-aircraft gunners claimed two more. For the second time Australian pilots reported the presence of Fw190s (actually the new clipped wing version of the Zero, code-named the Hamp).

On 25 August nine P-40s from No 75 Squadron went out in search of the barges on the western coast of Goodenough Island. After six runs over the beached barges, all seven were left burning. The main force of Japanese ships, ready to launch their assault on Milne, approached that night. Fittingly No 75 Squadron made the first offensive move with six Kittyhawks led by Turnbull, each dropping a 300lb bomb without success. RAAF Hudsons went in as well with their usual tenacity. Top cover was provided by six more Hawks led by Sqn Ldr Keith 'Bluey' Truscott, newly arrived to help Turnbull with No 76 Squadron.

Truscott was already somewhat of a legend among RAAF pilots with 15 victories in Spitfires while flying with No 452 Squadron

Below: **This is SV-S (A29-1134), a No 76 Squadron P-40N, at Labuan Island in 1945.** */Frank F. Smith via Bruce Hoy*

Above: **No 78 Squadron at Hollandia, 1944. Most single engine fighter units in New Guinea were required to carry white spinners, tails, wing leading edges for identification.**
/Frank F. Smith via Bruce Hoy

Right: **The first Allied fighter unit to land on Los Negros Island after its capture was No 76 Squadron. 12 Kittys landed on 8 March 1944, the day this photo was taken there. Note the severe defoliation as a result of the ground fighting. The P-40 in the foreground is SV-P, A29-337.**/*Bruce Hoy*

Below right: **No 78 Squadron with engines turning on Noemfoor Island, 1944. The first aircraft,** *El Toro,* **is HU-R (A29-401), a P-40N-1 belonging to Sqn Ldr Arch 'Curl the Mo' Simpson.**
/Frank F. Smith

96

out of England. A famous footballer before the war, he was almost washed out of flying school for lack of flying ability due to ham-handedness on the controls.

Between 0440 and 0530 hours Nos 75 and 76 Squadrons bombed and strafed the convoy, scoring two near misses on a transport and a direct hit on a corvette. Landings were made through the darkness and mist with the aid of a flare-path that could only be seen when circling low over the runway. One Kitty was lost but the pilot later rescued.

There was little sleep that night as, amidst the sound of Japanese gunfire, crews laboured in the mud to get the aircraft ready for the next day's battle. The Japanese had steamed into Milne Bay and disgorged a large number of troops and supplies before disappearing out to sea again.

The Kittys and Hudsons flew sortie after sortie, dropping bombs and strafing a bare six miles from the airstrip. The ground crews heard the entire action. No 75 Squadron alone flew 26 sorties. Jackson led two of the five attacks and Piper led two, destroying the important Japanese barges. The enemy continued to advance inland.

On the 27th the Japanese called in their own air power with eight dive bombers and 12 Zeros but they did little damage to No 1 Strip. Six Kittyhawks from No 75 Squadron met them, claiming 1-1-1. A week later three more enemy dive bombers were spotted crashed in the jungle. Two more Zeros were shot down as Jackson and Flt Sgt R. G. Riddel caught them after an attack on American Marauders. The only loss in these aerial combats was Flt Sgt S. Munro.

Later in the afternoon, enemy tanks were reported near KB Mission. Turnbull and Flt Lt R. C. Kerville took off about 1700 hours in search of the tanks and found a detachment of enemy troops. Turnbull pushed the nose down for a run and his Kittyhawk flicked over on its back at 200ft, diving straight into the ground. Turnbull's death only reinforced the fighting spirit of No. 76 Squadron as Truscott took his place as CO.

The next day the Japanese had advanced to within two miles of the airstrip and Kittys were barely off before beginning their runs. With the imminent fall of Milne Bay, all aircraft were ordered back to Moresby for the night after flying continual close support for the ground troops. Ground crews and troops were now fighting as a unit. Truscott himself stayed the night with a rifle, ready to defend the strip on the ground.

The next day the Kittyhawks returned and Truscott put them back into the fight with bombs and new machine gun barrels. By the first few days of September the Australians managed to turn back the Japanese attackers after a see-saw battle that almost resulted in

the taking of No 3 Strip on 31 August. The Kittyhawks flew continually throughout the campaign. By 5 September the enemy was in full retreat and late that night more Japanese ships came to shore, this time to pick up the survivors of the action and leave. The Japanese thus suffered their first major land defeat of the war at the hands of the tenacious Australians.

On the 7th the two Kittyhawk squadrons took part in the first attack from Milne Bay by RAAF Beaufighters, Beauforts and Hudsons against enemy shipping. This was the first combined operation of its kind mounted by the RAAF.

Tribute after tribute was given to the Aussies, especially the Kittyhawk squadrons. Maj-Gen C. Clowes, commander-in-chief of the forces at Milne Bay, wrote to Gen Blamey 'the action of 75 and 76 Squadrons RAAF in the first day was probably the decisive factor.' To this day the Milne Bay victory is looked upon by many as the battle that saved Australia. That the Hawks stayed in the air continually was a tribute to the ground crews who replaced 300 gun barrels in the course of the battle – the grit and mud often enlarged the bore from the normal .50 to .60cal! Flaps had to be replaced often due to the force of the water and mud thrown up on landing. No 75 Squadron maintenance officer, Flg Off W. I. Matson, served as the tireless ramrod behind most of the ground operations.

The two squadrons continued to fly ops until 21 September when relieved by the 35th and 36th FG, USAAF Airacobra units. No 75 Squadron went to Horn Island and No 76 to North-Western Area for rest and refitting.

A third Kittyhawk squadron, No 77, had been formed in March 1942 but it did not see action until flying in defence of North-Western Area in late September. On the 25th the Squadron's CO, R. Cresswell, fired the first bursts while trying to intercept night raiders. No 76 Squadron finally completed moving to this arena by October.

During the last week in November the Japanese carried out three heavy night raids on Darwin. No 77 Squadron had been trying to intercept the bombers but had no success until the 23rd when Cresswell downed one of the 18 bombers over the town that night.

The Japanese were not about to give up New Guinea and by the end of 1942 the RAAF Kittyhawk squadrons were slated to return to the fighting there as the first RAAF Spitfire squadrons formed a wing in North-Western Area. By February 1943 both No 75, under Sqn Ldr Wilfred S. Arthur, and No 77, still under Cresswell, were flying from Milne Bay.

By May 1943 Japanese Adm Yamamoto

was determined to regain his now shattered air superiority over New Guinea. On 14 May, when Milne Bay was attacked, Nos 75 and 77 Squadrons went up against a total of 37 Bettys, eight Vals and over 20 Zeros. Sqn Ldr Arthur placed the 15 Kittys up-sun and the Aussies shot down four bombers, two fighters and probably five more bombers for the loss of one pilot. Arthur, with jammed guns, led the P-40s in five attacks with a ferocity that drove him to slice away at the tail of a Val with his propeller regardless of the rear gunner's fire. He was awarded a DSO on the spot. This battle turned out to be the last major encounter for Australian fighter pilots in the Pacific war.

As Allied air operations shifted consistently to the offensive, more RAAF Kittyhawk squadrons were formed. Nos 84 and 86 Squadrons, assigned to defend the Merauke-Torres Strait, saw little action except for 22 and 23 January 1944 when two Bettys and a Zero were destroyed. The enemy never returned.

Nos 75, 76 and 77 Squadrons were formed into No 73 Wing, based on Kiriwina Island. Their primary mission was dive-bombing against targets on Basmata, Jacquinot Bay and over the entire length of New Britain. Just before American troops hit Cape Gloucester on 26 December 1943, No 73 Wing mustered 63 P-40s against the airstrip and supply depots at Gasmata. The Kittys returned on 12 January as Nos 76 and 78 Squadrons pounded the base into a burning mass of rubble.

In March 1944, with the conquest of the Admiralty Islands, Rabaul was left to shrivel up due to lack of supplies. Nos 76, 77 and 79 Squadrons were transferred to the Admiralties to serve as air defence but not a single Japanese aircraft showed up. After covering the US landings, the three squadrons flew boring convoy escort for the rest of their stay.

From the first time No 75 Squadron was sent to Moresby, the Kittyhawk pilots were held in reverence by the Australian ground forces and vice versa. Kittys were assigned ground support for most of their operations in the RAAF. Nos 75, 78 and 80 Squadrons flew out of Nadzab, near Lae, to support Australian forces and cover the Allied landings in April at Hollandia. On 3 June 1944 No 78 Squadron fought their only air combat as eight pilots shot down nine Japanese aircraft out of a formation of 12 Oscars and three Kates. When the fight was over after 40 minutes there was only one pilot missing. The engagement was significant for two reasons: it established a record in the RAAF and it turned out to be the last air to air combat fought by the RAAF.

The Americans fought the rest of the air war to the north as the Australians continued to island hop in support of those on the ground, often flying the more dangerous missions of low-level attack. But to the Aussies who flew them, their Kittys were dearly loved and flown in greater numbers than any other fighter in the RAAF. The last of the 842 Kittyhawks delivered to the RAAF operated out of Borneo as late as 23 July 1945. Nos 75, 78 and 80 Squadrons flew their P-40s in this area on police duties until the surrender with Japan was signed. Bluey Truscott ended up the leading RAAF ace with 17 victories and he might have scored further but he was killed in a tragic flying accident on 28 March 1943 while making mock attacks on a Catalina.

Australia also acquired 67 P-40Ns for Dutch pilots flying in No 120 (Netherlands East Indies) Squadron. Formed on 10 December 1943, the Squadron was attached to the RAAF at Potshot in western Australia, The Dutch pilots had been trained at a joint Dutch Army-Navy flying school in Jackson, Missouri that had been set up after the collapse of resistance in both the Netherlands and the East Indies. Of the 334 trained pilots, 67 were moved on to fighters and by 31 December No 120 Squadron had 13

Above and right: **Australia acquired 67 P-40Ns for the Dutch flying in No 120 Netherlands East Indies Squadron. The unit flew from Merauke, Netherlands New Guinea but did not see much action until transferred to Noemfoor, Biak, New Guinea. The Dutch kept their Kittys until 1949.**/*Frank F. Smith*

P-40Ns, 23 NEI officers and five RAAF officers at Canberra.

The squadron became operational in April, flying from Merauke, Netherlands New Guinea, in the ground support role but very little action was seen until the unit was transferred to Noemfoor, near Biak. Intense bombing and strafing resulted in heavy losses before the end of the war with Japan.

Retaining their P-40Ns, No 120 Squadron was transferred to Surabaya, Java in November 1946. By May they were operating out of Semarang where they again flew combat against Indonesian rebels. Early in 1948 the Dutch took their Kittys to Andir and flew their last missions in December in support of the Dutch landings at Djocja. When the Armistice was signed in July 1949, No 120 Squadron had 11 Kittyhawks flying, certainly the last to see combat anywhere.

As the Japanese stormed through the Pacific with one victory after the other in late 1941 and early 1942, the Dominion

of New Zealand presented a ripe target for conquest. As with the Australians, New Zealanders had served throughout the RAF but special consideration was given to forming Royal New Zealand Air Force units. After No 75 Squadron (bombers) came into being, No 485 Squadron formed flying fighters. Several RNZAF units operated in Europe, as did their RAAF counterparts, alongside the Allies, but it was not until late 1941 that the first all-New Zealand unit, No 488 Squadron, formed in the Far East flying Brewster Buffaloes.

As the Buffaloes were decimated by the superior Japanese fighters in the early Pacific fighting, consideration was given to re-equipping the RNZAF with P-40E Kittyhawks that had originally been earmarked for Britain. No 14 Squadron was formed in April 1942 from what was left of No 488. In May 80 Kittyhawks were promised to New Zealand and by June a second and third Kitty squadron, Nos 15 and 16, were in

existence. With July came 44 of the Kittys, enough to get the three squadrons operational and to form No 2 Fighter Operational Training Unit. As it turned out, only 62 of the P-40Es ever arrived.

By August 1942 and the invasion of Guadalcanal by the Americans, the action was most definitely shifting into an increasing offensive by the Allies. Midway, the Coral Sea and Milne Bay had been Allied victories and the Solomons were looked upon as needing support. Late in October No 15 Squadron RNZAF was sent to Tonga to take over the P-40Ks of the 68th FS (USAAF) in the role of air defence. For three and a half months Sqn Ldr A. Crichton led the well worn P-40s

on anti-submarine patrols without seeing any action.

By April 1943 No 14 Squadron went to Espiritu Santo to take over the air defence mission from the Americans. In the same month the RNZAF began to arrive on Guadalcanal to aid the numerous US squadrons defending the island. By the 26th No 15 Squadron arrived flying No 14's newer P-40Ms. The Squadron was led by Michael Herrick who had five German aircraft to his credit as a night fighter pilot in the RAF. On 6 May Herrick made the first New Zealand fighter victory by shooting down a Zero.

On 8 May No 15 Squadron flew its first bomber escort, joining 32 Marine F4U

Corsairs as Dauntlesses and Avengers went after three Japanese destroyers. Throughout the Kiwis' time on 'the Canal' it was not unusual to see their Kittys teamed up with P-38s, P-39s, other P-40s, F4Us and F4Fs on missions.

As Allied air power grew in strength, the Japanese countered by sending in more fighter groups. On 7 June 1943 around 50 enemy fighters were bounced between Buraku and the Russells by 104 Allied fighters, 12 from No 15 Squadron. The fight lasted for 90 minutes and 23 Zeros were claimed, four falling to the Kiwis. Four of the Kiwi Kittyhawks were damaged but no one was lost.

On 12 June No 14 Squadron flew in to relieve No 15 but not before another large enemy air raid in which No 14's pilots shot down six. Flg Off K. P. C. Morpeth was lost, the first New Zealand fighter pilot to be killed in action. No 14 Squadron continued to be in the thick of the action in the Solomons, giving and taking but mostly taking, before moving on to New Georgia and Munda in late June.

On 4 July eight of the Squadron's Kittyhawks were patrolling Rendova at 14,000ft when surprised by over 40 enemy aircraft. For over an hour the badly split up Kiwis tangled with their assailants. Flg Off G. B. Fisken managed to down two Zeros and a Betty, the latter turning out to be the only multi-engine kill made by the RNZAF. The action brought his score to five over the Solomons and another six which he shot down over Singapore in early 1942, making him New Zealand's top scorer against the Japanese.

A fourth Kittyhawk squadron, No 17, had been formed the previous October. This freed No 16 Squadron to base out of Santo in June 1943 and finally replace No 14 Squadron on Guadalcanal by 25 July. No 17 then flew in to Santo to allow No 14's pilots a well deserved rest at home. No 16 Squadron's debut was a rough one on 31 July when 30 Zeros bounced the Kiwis after the latter had completed a bomber escort. Two Kittys and one pilot were lost. Regardless, the squadron went on to rack up nine kills in August, flying its last combat of the tour on 3 September.

Nos 15 and 17 Squadrons flew up to Guadalcanal to take No 16 Squadron's place. Close bomber escort was the assignment, meaning that the other units flying loose fighter escort were to see air to air combat for a while. The Kiwis were particularly popular with American bomber crews due to their determination to stick with the heavies at all times. But the New Zealanders did manage to engage the enemy in late September and October, gaining a number of kills.

As Allied victory carried the action on up the island chain, an RNZAF base was set up on Ondonga, Nos 15 and 18 Squadrons forming a wing and No 17 Squadron moving to Santo. The Kiwis were a part of the 660 aircraft available to support the Bougainville landings and action was resumed on 27 October as the Kittys covered the Treasury Island landings. On 1 November No 18 Squadron claimed seven kills and one probable out of the 50 or 60 Zeros encountered over the Empress Augusta Bay landings. The RNZAF Fighter Wing continued to give bomber escort and patrol during November and December over Bougainville, flying over 1,000 sorties in November alone. Several claims were made against the opposing Japanese fighters and dive bombers.

Above: **A No 76 Squadron Kitty on Morotai warms up for, most likely, a convoy or shipping patrol since this was the unit's primary task in 1944.**
[RAAF via Barry Pattison

Right: **Wg Cdr Geoff Atherton leads No 80 Squadron on a fighter-bomber mission to the Halmaheras in his** *Cleopatra III,* **BU-B (A29-629). An accountant before the war, he claimed 2½ victories with No 75 Squadron over New Guinea and finished the war with five victories.**
/Barry Pattison

Above: **Wg Cdr Geoff Atherton's P-40N (ex-USAAF 43-22854), No 80 Squadron, 78 Wing, being serviced at Wama Strip, Morotai in early 1945. Shortly afterward, on 3 February 1945, Atherton was shot down by ground fire. Ditching near the Japanese, he waited in shark infested water and was finally picked up by a Catalina.**
/RAAF via Frank F. Smith

Now that Rabaul was within range of fighter strikes, the New Zealanders put up 24 Kittys, led by Wg Cdr Trevor Freeman, as a part of the 80 fighters staging through Bougainville on 17 December to hit the now isolated target. Nos 15 and 18 Squadrons had relieved 14 and 16 Squadrons as the units in the wing and they pounced back into action by tangling with the intercepting Zeros. Although Freeman and another pilot were lost, the Kiwis got five of the nine kills claimed. Wg Cdr C. W. K. Nicholls, a Battle of France veteran, arrived to command the wing in February 1944.

By mid-December 1943 No 17 Squadron was back in the picture, relieving No 14. On 24 December, 24 RNZAF Kittys joined 24 American fighters to sweep Rabaul. Two groups of 20 Zeros each rose to meet the incoming fighters. Sqn Ldr J. H. Arkwright led No 16 Squadron on the nearest formation and Sqn Ldr R. G. H. Newton took No 17 Squadron after the other. After Newton got a Zero, the New Zealanders got into a milling fight that proved to be the roughest of the war so far.

Newton got two more A6Ms and started to climb to rejoin when he was jumped by six Zeros. Back down to just over the sea they roared and Newton joined on another Kitty, both scissoring for mutual support as they headed for the rally point over Cape St George and four orbiting Kittyhawks. It was in vain – another six Zeros forced the two Kiwis apart. Newton then found another P-40 to scissor with but the new wingman was shot down. Newton finally evaded his pursuers and made it back to base alone.

The action turned out to be the record for the wing – 12 kills, four probables and several damaged. Unfortunately it cost seven Kittys and five pilots.

As the next few weeks went by, the wing participated in every major attack on Rabaul from the Solomons, escorting both the B-24s and the Navy SBDs and TBFs. A detachment from No 17 Squadron was flying from Torokina as well, later joined by the entire unit and by No 15 Squadron, the latter

commanded by J. A. A. Gibson, another ace with 13½ kills gained in the RAF.

Encounters with the enemy were made throughout January, getting 15 for the loss of five pilots. Newton made two of the kills, elevating him into the rank of ace. Rabaul remained the primary target as the Allies totally encircled it.

On 22 January, No 18 Squadron entered the theatre for its second combat tour, replacing No 17 Squadron. After one more attack on Vunakanau airfield near Rabaul while escorting TBFs (the wing got two Zeros

Below: **No 80 Squadron P-40Ns in flight, 1945.** */Frank Folmer via Frank F. Smith*

Bottom: **A No 80 Squadron Kittyhawk, a former USAAF P-40N, 1945.** */Frank Folmer via Frank F. Smith*

for the loss of a Kitty), the RNZAF Wing began flying cover for the 15 February 1944 landings on Green Island.

After the Japanese pulled their entire air force out of Rabaul in February (70 aircraft of the 1,000 stationed on the island since 1942 and 1943 were all that remained), air strikes were launched to destroy what supplies remained. On 10 March, 24 Kiwi Kittyhawks

returned with 500lb bombs. These P-40s had the honour of flying the first fighter-bomber sorties against Rabaul three days earlier and were repeating the performance. By 20 March the encirclement of New Ireland and New Britain was complete but the Japanese forces remaining around Bougainville launched a counter-offensive. By 21 March the New Zealanders were carrying 1,000lb bombs on their Kittyhawks to repulse the attack, along with Navy SBDs and TBFs.

A new Kittyhawk squadron, No 19 replaced No 18 Squadron at Torokina to join in the attacks against Rabaul with No 14 Squadron, and a system of two RNZAF squadrons rotating every six weeks was established. A seventh Kitty unit, No 20 Squadron, had been formed in New Zealand, but by the time it arrived on Bougainville for its first tour on 14 May 1944, it had been re-equipped with Corsairs. Soon, all the remaining RNZAF fighter squadrons transitioned to the Corsair.

So, the day of the Kiwi Kittys was over. They had destroyed 99 enemy aircraft and, pleased though they were with the Corsair, the New Zealanders never added that final aerial victory to bring their score to 100.

Actually, there was still another Kittyhawk squadron over New Guinea. It was the 35th FS of the 49th FG which flew Kittyhawk Mk Is for a time in a sort of reverse Lend-Lease arrangement. This resulted from an RAAF/USAAF pool in Australia from which Allied air forces in that theatre were supplied.

Above: **The No 80 Squadron P-40N belonging to Flg Off E. 'Honey' Faine.** /*Frank Folmer via Frank F. Smith*

Right: **Sqn Ldr John Waddy on the cockpit sill of his No 80 Squadron P-40N-35, (A29-1137), at Morotti, 1945. The 'VE' below the German and Italian victory markings stand for victory in Europe.**/*Frank F. Smith*

Above: **In April 1942 the first New Zealand Kittyhawk squadron, No 14 Squadron, was formed out of the battered remnants of No 488 Squadron, a Buffalo unit. P-40Es destined for Britain were diverted for the RNZAF. Here two of the P-40Es, HQ-B (NZ3008)** *Umslopogaas* **in the foreground, of No 14 Squadron cruise by, January 1943.**/*Frank F. Smith*

Left: **P-40Ns from No 82 Squadron at Labuan Island, North Borneo in 1945.**/*Frank F. Smith*

Above: **Another No 14 Squadron P-40E, RNZAF, serial no NZ3007, January 1943.**/*Frank F. Smith*

Left: **Two more Royal New Zealand Air Force squadrons, Nos 15 and 16, were formed after No 14 before any Kittys arrived. In July 1942 44 P-40Es arrived to get the three units, along with No 2 Fighter Operational Training Unit, operational. This P-40E-1-CU, NZ3039, of No 15 Squadron is flying over Auckland in late 1943. Note the early British insignia and camouflage.**/*Frank F. Smith*

Below left: **Another RNZAF No 15 Squadron P-40E (NZ3040) over the North Cape area in 1942 before the change in markings.** /*Frank F. Smith*

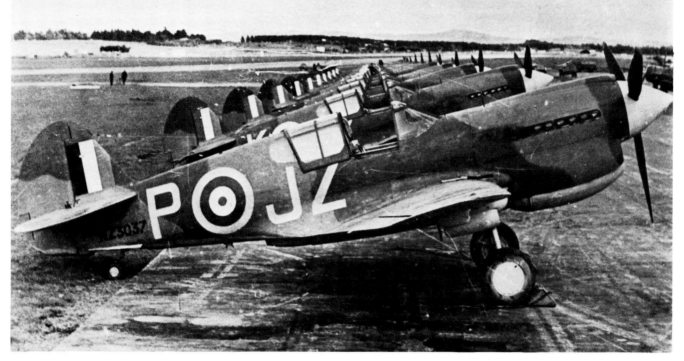

Above: **Here No 15 Squadron's P-40Es are lined up at Whenupai, New Zealand after equipping with the newly arrived fighters.** */Frank F. Smith*

Below: **No 16 was the third New Zealand squadron to work up on the Kitty, receiving a share of the P-40Es earmarked for Britain. These No 16** Squadron Kittyhawk IAs are seen during operational training in the summer of 1942. Note the change in markings. The idea was to reduce the red centre to avoid confusion with the Japanese inline fighters. */Frank F. Smith*

Above: **A P-40K (NZ3055) of No 14 Squadron, 1943.**
/Frank F. Smith

Right: **This P-40K of No 14 Squadron, RNZAF, is resting on Norfolk Island in 1943.**
/Frank F. Smith

Below right: **New Zealand Kittys eventually adopted their own form of markings for recognition purposes, consisting of a series of red bordered white stripes on the wings and tail and in front of as well as behind the cockpit. White spinners were added and the fin flash reduced in width.**
/Frank F. Smith

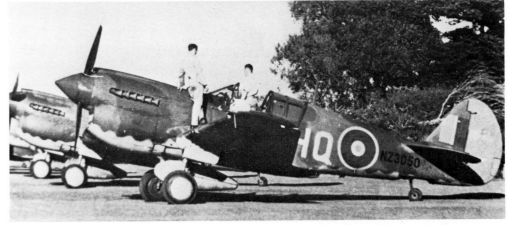

Above: **Another shot of** *Gloria Lyons*, **a Kittyhawk Mk IV (P-40N-1) in the Solomons, 1944. Note 2½ kill flags and the numerous bomb symbols. The Kitty may have been Flg Off C. D. A. Highet's of No 18 Squadron. Note the bars on the national markings, and the white tails and spinners.**
/R. C. Jones via Chris Shores

Right: **A rare shot—A P-40E in Japanese markings. The Japanese captured so many Kittyhawks on Java that some were used to equip a provisional interceptor outfit which operated in the defence of Rangoon for a short time in 1943. The Dutch left crates and crates of Kittys in their retreat and about a dozen were found in various states of damage or disassembly. This photo was taken at Andir Airfield, Bandoeng, May 1942, just before the Japanese ferried the P-40 out for evaluation.**
/Osamu Tagaya

Below right: **Another of the Kittys captured by the Japanese at Andir Airfield, Bandoeng, Java from the Dutch. Note the rectangular national insignia and the Brewster Buffalo and B-17 in the background. Two more P-40Es were captured intact on Mindanao, Philippines. Maj Charles Sneed, USAAF, was temporarily taken out of captivity by the Japanese to teach the Japanese to fly them and he ended up being the ferry pilot for the aircraft as well. After being placed back in captivity, he was killed by a US airstrike on a POW troopship in 1944 against Takao Harbour, Taiwan.**
/Osamu Tagaya

7 US P-40s in the Pacific

Not until mid-1942 were the Allies able to employ anything but stop-gap measures to slow Japan's series of conquests in the Pacific. The Battle of Midway on 4 June changed everything. Within the space of perhaps 200 human heartbeats 37 US Navy SBD Dauntless dive bombers from two US Fleet carriers so damaged the Imperial Japanese Navy that it never recovered; and for the first time Allied planners could think about offensive action in the Pacific.

Even as the Battle of Midway was being fought, Gen George C. Kenney was piecing together the US 5th Air Force in Australia. He would depend upon Kittyhawks for the bulk of his tactical fighter force, especially during the early, toughest fighting – Dutch, RNZAF and RAAF Kittyhawks – along with the Warhawks (and Kittyhawks) of the US 49th FG. The 5th Air Force would fight with Gen Douglas MacArthur from New Guinea to the Philippines.

The 9th FS of the 49th FG was equipped with Kittyhawk Mk Is from March 1942 until it began receiving P-38s in January 1943. The rest of the group would keep their Warhawks until November 1943 when the entire group transferred to P-47s. Still later, the group would be re-equipped with P-38s. By the end of the war, the 49th FG would be well known indeed; but records of its actions during the early days, when the 49'ers met superior numbers of the enemy in the air with their well-worn Hawks, are today either incomplete or missing altogether. They fought from Horn Island, Port Darwin and New Guinea with their Hawks, mostly against Japanese Navy Zeros ('Zekes') of the Japanese 25th and 26th Air Flotillas.

Meanwhile, the US 7th Air Force had risen from the ashes of the Hawaiian Air Force at Pearl Harbor. It contained two Warhawk groups: the 15th FG, two squadrons of which remained on duty in Hawaii until February 1945, while its 45th FS flew to Baker Island in September 1943; and the 318th FG which would accompany Adm Chester Nimitz' forces across the central Pacific via the Gilberts, Marshalls, Marianas, Carolines, and Palaus to the Philippines.

The US 13th Air Force, formed in New Caledonia in January 1943, gained the 347th FG, one squadron of which was Warhawk-equipped, and the 44th FS of the 18th FG flying P-40Fs. The 13th Air Force, commanded by Gen Nathan Twining (later Gen Hubert Harmon), joined the Navy and Marine air forces in the campaign for the Solomon Islands, New Georgia, Bougainville and Rabaul.

Sgt Henry J. Straub was a crew chief with the 44th FS:

'I arrived at Wheeler Field on 13 December, 1939, assigned to the 19th PS of the 18th PG, then commanded by Maj Clyde K. Rich. Later, I was reassigned to the 78th Squadron until the 44th Squadron was organised at Bellows Field in June 1942.

'Perhaps I should explain that the original 44th Squadron, part of the 15th PG formed early in 1941 at Wheeler Field, later became the 339th FS and was sent to Christmas and Canton Islands. They came to Guadalcanal as the 339th Night Fighter Squadron flying P-70s (converted A-20s). The 339th belonged to the 347th FG by that time, and later received some P-38s and P-39s.

'The formation of the 44th Squadron at Bellows was partly accomplished by drawing on personnel from the four squadrons of the 18th group which then consisted of the 6th, 19th and 78th FSs, along with the 26th Attack Squadron and the Headquarters Squadron. The balance of the personnel was made up of new pilots and recruits from stateside.

'After training at Bellows, which was then being greatly enlarged, the 44th packed up and 12 of our Warhawks were loaded on the aircraft carrier USS *Nassau*. The rest of the aircraft were put aboard the plane carrier USS *Kitty Hawk*, which was a converted Great Lakes train carrier. An advance cadre of pilots and men were flown to New Caledonia by C-47 troop carriers en route to Australia.

'I left Hickam Field in Hawaii in October 1942. Our C-47 flew by way of Christmas, Canton and Fiji Islands, then on to New Caledonia. After about two weeks at Tontuta Airbase, some 20 miles north of Noumea,

Right: **Rare photo, dated 4 June 1942, of one of the Carrier** *Yorktown's* **SBDs preparing to take-off on the eve of the Battle of Midway. On this day the unremarkable Dauntless would be the most significant aeroplane in the world.**/*US Navy*

Above: **One of the 9th FS's Kittyhawks, RAF serial ET735.**/*Frank F Smith*

we boarded the USS *Nassau* in Noumea Harbour and sailed north for two days. On the afternoon of the third day, after a submarine attack, we launched the aircraft.

'The Navy F4F Wildcats went off first, followed by the SBD Dauntlesses and the F6F Hellcats, then the TBF Avengers. As we readied the 12 P-40F Warhawks, we discovered that the engines were running rough. The Marines had been turning them up at 900rpm and checking magnetos at 1,400rpm. Being a Packard Rolls-Royce engine, they should have been turned at 1,400rpm and checked out at 2,750rpm. We had no spare plugs available, so we leaned-out the mixtures and tried to burn-off the deposits on the plugs, hoping for enough rpm and horsepower to get the Hawks off the deck.

'Our aircraft were spotted forward of the aft elevator leaving about 300ft for take-off. The ship was probably going at full speed which was around 10 knots (the USS *Nassau* was a converted Liberty Ship with a flight deck). It was a warm day and there was not much wind across the deck. The major went off first, followed by the others. Then my plane, No 104, took-off with 1-Lt Robert

Westbrook at the controls. When he turned up the engine to check the magnetos it spat and sputtered, but Westy sailed down the deck and disappeared under the ship's bow. I can still hear that engine. I ran to the port side of the ship and saw Westy skimming over the whitecaps, but gaining speed every second. He finally raised his nose and climbed for altitude. As he made his climbing turn, he dived the carrier deck and roared over so low some of the seamen fell flat on their stomachs.

'The USS *Nassau* put into harbour at Espirito Santo and we were taken ashore by Higgins Boat. An Army division was there, awaiting transport north to relieve the Marines on Guadalcanal. Their ship had sunk after hitting one of our own mines in the harbour. Trucks took us halfway around the island to the bomber strip. We were given some tents and assigned an area close to our aircraft. All the planes were dispersed throughout the surrounding jungle.

'We were there a week or two and our planes flew some routine patrols. Just before we left it was learned that the enemy was sending a large convoy from Rabaul to reinforce their troops on Guadalcanal. Our Air Force brought in some B-25 Mitchells and B-26 Marauders, the Marauders fitted with torpedos.

'It was a long flight up north and back, more than 600 miles. On the day they took off, the B-17 Fortresses were first, followed by the TBFs, B-25s, the B-26s and the Black Cats. The B-17s that came back were really shot up, and a couple of B-25s made it back. I don't remember any B-26s returning; the range was too great. The Black Cats picked up crews that had to ditch.

'The *Kitty Hawk* then arrived with our P-40s and P-39s. To get the aircraft ashore, a channel had been blasted through the coral reef, and steel cubicles bolted together to make a barge which was powered by a 25hp

Johnson outboard engine. Three men rode the barge out to the *Kitty Hawk* and put alongside in rough water. It was a very risky undertaking. The ship swung each plane over the side by cargo boom, then we secured it and took it ashore. Some dunnage was placed on the sand as a cargo ramp and Cletracs were used to pull the barges up near the taxiway.

'The remainder of the squadron had left Hawaii on a Liberty Ship and arrived at Vila on Efate, an island to the south of us which was also in the New Hebrides. The airfield there was occupied by a Navy squadron with Joe Foss commanding. We flew from there for a short time then moved across the island into the jungle on a strip just completed by the SeaBees. We were cut off from the rest of the world.

'On Efate, we flew patrols and trained pilots. About three days before Christmas 1942 four of our planes were on a routine mission when they ran into a storm. They spotted an island and, being short of fuel, made belly landings in a clearing on the island of Erromango. I was one of 18 men who went on the expedition to recover those aircraft. There was an Australian coast watcher there, and our people had landed almost at his doorstep.

'In early January 1943 our first group of pilots and support personnel deployed to Guadalcanal. Our troops had been fighting there since the previous August, and it had taken that long to defeat the enemy there. Six major naval engagements had been fought off Guadalcanal, and there had been a lot of air battles. Now, the 44th FS and our P-40Fs were to go into combat.

'I was bumped off the C-47 I was supposed to take and caught another one. Just south of Guadalcanal, near San Cristabel, we saw the C-47 from which I was bumped burning on the beach. Then some of our Warhawks came alongside to escort us in. We landed at Henderson Field and were taken to my squadron area on Fighter One at Lunga Beach. I had arrived in a secure area, I was told – and we were bombed every day for the next 68 days!

'Fighter One Base at Lunga Beach was taken from the enemy over Christmas Week and we shared it with a Marine fighter squadron known as the "Black Sheep", VMF-214, equipped with F4U Corsairs. They were at one end of the field and we at the other. There was one small runway from which planes normally took-off from east to west. We had Marine artillery around the field perimeter, with anti-aircraft positions on the beach.

'The motion picture area on the field drew lots of off-duty personnel each night but it often took hours to complete a film because

of the bombing. Some nights, the movie would begin at 2100 hours and would not be completed until 0300 hours the following morning.

'We started operations flying bomber escort. The targets were Munda on New Georgia, Vella la Vella and Bougainville. We usually put up 16 planes with two spares on stand-by. As a rule, one of the spares took-off with the flight and if all aircraft were okay for go, the spare would turn back. If anyone had trouble, he would turn back and the spare would take his place. Our pilots flew two-plane elements patterned after a tactic proven by Chennault's Flying Tigers.

'Since I cannot remember dates, I can only recall for you some of those incidents that impressed me at the time, some relatively unimportant, perhaps, but which reflect the atmosphere at Fighter One. For example, one morning about daylight as I was turning-up my aircraft, a Navy F4F Wildcat was taking-off. He was in trouble and hit the top of the trees. We could hear the crash, and smoke and flames soared above the jungle. After a while, a young Navy pilot walked by

Top: **Kittyhawk s/n ET614 of the 9th FS, 49th FG.**
/Frank F. Smith

Above: **A nice, tight formation of 9th FS Kittys.**
/Frank F. Smith

with his parachute tucked under his arm. I asked him about the plane that crashed and he acknowledged that it was his, but said as a result he would not miss breakfast of pancakes and eggs that morning.

'The living conditions there were not the best. The food was rotten and the desalinated sea water was worse. Everyone had the "GIs" (diarrhoea). It was tough on us, but worse for the pilots. Sleep was hard to get. During one of the enemy bombings, we lost Lt Tabor. He hit another plane head-on while chasing a Zero. Every time our planes went out, the score grew higher and higher because the Allies were driving further north. Munda was knocked out of action and Vella la Vella was becoming useless to the Japanese.

'Every day a Japanese reconnaissance plane would fly over, but we no longer blew the alert signal because the troops were injuring themselves jumping into holes. Once in a while we would send a fighter up to wait for him, but I don't think they ever got him. Then at night, "Washing Machine Charley" came over, scattered a few eggs and went home. Of course, we were doing the same thing to the enemy, though on a larger scale.

'One day, a New Zealand Kittyhawk squadron moved in. One of their flight officers had fought at night in England during the Blitz. He was Flg Off Ray W. Stuart. He and Capt Robert Westbrook, who flew my No 104 Warhawk, went up after Charley one night, in fact they tried for three nights, but the glare from the P-40's exhaust stacks blinded them and they were not successful.

'On the next full moon, however, Maj Kettle of the 339th FS, by then equipped with P-38s, went up. When the searchlights bracketed the enemy craft it turned out to be a six-engine flying boat. Kettle made three passes at it and we could see his tracers as one engine and the outboard portion of the enemy's wing broke away. Charley crashed about 20 miles north, towards Cape Esperance. After that, the 339th flew a routine night flight with P-38s.

'We lost Doc Wheaton as a result of an air battle over Bougainville. His Warhawk was badly damaged. He was able to make it back as far as Rendora, but crashed into the

Below: **Crew of Capt Westbrook's Warhawk, (left to right) John Gorman, Henry Straub and George Dixer, 7 June 1943, Guadalcanal.**/*Henry Straub*

Bottom: **Oil from an exploding Zeke sprayed this Warhawk of the 7th FS, 49th FG. One crewman wipes away oil while others rearm. Dobodura, New Guinea, May 1943.**/*USAF*

water about half a mile short of the runway. He was seen getting out of the aircraft and standing on the wing. By the time the crash boat reached the site, however, they could not find him. The barracuda probably did.'

Late in February 1943 a US Army division took the Russell Island, 35 miles north-west of Guadalcanal, without opposition. This firmly established the Allies in the Solomons, and the drive to defeat the enemy on Rabaul had begun. The Japanese, however, were determined to hold Rabaul, and to reinforce their positions on New Guinea and the Solomons. Their attempt in March 1943 to send a large convoy to Lae in New Guinea resulted in the Battle of the Bismarck Sea and the loss of over 3,500 men along with

Below: **Another Warhawk of the 7th FS prepares for take-off at Dobodura.**/*USAF*

Bottom: **A K-model Warhawk of the 7th FS gassing-up at Dobo.**/*USAF*

much irreplaceable shipping and many aircraft. Just a month later, Rabaul-based aircraft, aided by carrier planes from Truk, sought to knock out Allied airpower in the Solomons, but this effort also cost the enemy dearly, and in late June Allied forces under MacArthur landed on islands off eastern New Guinea and on the New Guinea coast north-west of Buna. At about the same time Allied forces in the Solomons landed on New Georgia in the central Solomons, while stepping up their attacks on Bougainville.

The Japanese defended New Georgia and Bougainville stoutly. The Munda airfield on New Guinea was captured in August, but the island group was not secured until October. On 1 November Bougainville was invaded, but not until late that month was the beachhead at Empress Augusta Bay secured.

Mr Straub continues:

'Lt Head was lost over Bougainville and that was a very big loss to the squadron. Lt Jack Bade was one of our aces. He came back one day after a raid on Bougainville pretty badly shot up. He had taken a 20mm round in the cockpit near his right foot. Jack's foot and leg were full of shrapnel, and a bullet had creased his forehead. There was a lot of blood when we pulled him from the cockpit after his belly landing, but he recovered quickly and returned to duty.

'On the morning of the landings at New Georgia, all our fighters were preparing for take-off. The P-38s and the F4Us were to take off from east to west, and the P-40s and

Below: **In February 1944 these P-40N-5s of the 7th FS, 49th FG, were at Cape Gloucester, New Britain, wearing the white tails adopted by the RAAF and RNZAF for the theatre.**/*USAF*

Bottom: **P-40F of the 44th FS, 18th FG, on the fighter strip at Henderson Field, Guadalcanal, June 1943.** /*USMC*

P-39s from west to east. All of the planes were bunched up at each end of the field. The P-38s went first. Eleven planes were airborne when the next P-38 lifted-off and did a complete roll, nosed down, exploded and slid into four P-39s waiting to take-off. The P-38 was carrying a 175gal belly tank and two 500lb bombs. The fuel tank ruptured and engulfed the Airacobras in flames. The bombs did not explode. Sgt Ray Parkhurst and some other Airacobra crews somehow managed to save two of the P-39 pilots. Two others died along with the Lightning pilot.

'We continued to launch aircraft until all were up, and when they returned we serviced them and put them up again. Our aircraft flew three strikes that day, the last of them returning after dark.

'On 7 June our intelligence officer informed us that 125 enemy aircraft had taken-off from Rabaul. They were sure to penetrate our fighter screen and we knew approximately when to expect them. I saw Lt Jack Bade off in No 104, then joined other support personnel to watch from the beach.

'The first thing I saw was five Japanese dive bombers diving on the Navy base at Tulgi and a P-39 closing fast from above which started with the last one and went right on down the line shooting down all five in one pass. Out in the channel, between Guadalcanal and Tulgi, a US destroyer, I believe it was the USS *Ward*, was hit by an enemy dive bomber. There was one big orange flash and the destroyer disappeared! All hands were lost. The sky was full of planes; there were dogfights all over the place. Then, two of our aircraft buzzed the

field so we ran back to the service area. It didn't matter which crew was responsible for a given P-40 during such action; everyone helped to refuel and reload the guns. The engine was quickly checked for hits and the oil level checked. Someone would give the pilot a drink of water, then we'd cheer him off again. "Go! Go! Good luck, Lieutenant!"

'Just as those first two P-40's took-off to return to the fight, someone shouted, "Look out! Zero!"

'I had seen this one approaching from the north over the trees, but I thought it was a Navy F4F. The Zero made a strafing run on us, but there was indeed an F4F right on his tail. I ran like mad for the bunker, dived in head-first, and landed on two friends from back home. Some reunion.

Above: **Lt Jack Bade was 44th FS ace with seven victories.**
|*Henry Straub*

Left: Phebe **was a 44th FS Merlin-powered Warhawk; Guadalcanal, 1943.**
|*Henry Straub*

Top: **Warhawk 104, Westbrook's machine, and crew chief Henry Straub.** /*Henry Straub*

Top right: **The 44th FS's scoreboard on Guadalcanal was soon filled and a second one begun.**/*Henry Straub*

Above: **The 44th also adopted white tails and diagonal wing stripes early in 1944.** /*Henry Straub*

Right: **Six major naval engagements were fought off Guadalcanal, and there were countless air strikes against enemy shipping by Allied land-based aircraft. Here, an enemy ship burns after being hit by USAAF planes from Henderson Field.** /*USAF*

'During the Munda landing on New Georgia, Capt Westbrook, flying my No 104, took a hit in the electrical system and the cockpit filled up with smoke. But Westy opened the canopy and flew the plane back with his head outside the cockpit.

'Since we had the wrecked P-40 that Jack Bade had brought home all shot up, I stripped the wiring harness from it and installed it in No 104. Three long days I stood on my head in 140° temperatures to install that wiring. Then, just a few days later a Lt Winchester was flying No 104 and was forced to bail out after taking a burst of fire from another P-40 while inside a cloud. That was the end of No 104. The enemy had been unable to get her in countless air battles; she had to go in an accident, and without Capt Westbrook at the controls.

'I was relieved in October 1943 and went to New Zealand for rest. When I returned, the squadron was trading its Warhawks for P-38s. The Lightning, too, was a fine aeroplane, and the 44th FS added many more proud pages to its record while flying it.'

In the end, Rabaul was not taken by direct assault. The triple-pronged Allied offensive came together to encircle the 100,000 enemy there. Cut off from supply, their aircraft gone, their fleet unable to relieve them, the Japanese on Rabaul were simply by-passed and left to sit out the war impotently.

By the time the campaign for the Philippines began on 20 October 1944, the Hawks had done their job in the Pacific and had been replaced by P-47s, P-51s and P-38s, the latter being especially suited to operations in that theatre because of its greater range, and the security its two engines provided to its pilots over those long stretches of water. But in the early days, when there was only a handful of P-38s in the Pacific – and a skyful of the enemy – it was the Kittyhawks and Warhawks that provided the sharpest edge of the Allies' aerial sword in defence of Australia, and over New Guinea and the Solomons.

'Later, when things quietened down and we got our planes serviced and secured, we learned that the coast watcher reported that only two or three cripples made it back to Rabaul. The 44th FS got its share of the kills. Lt Bade, flying No 104 Warhawk, was officially credited with three Zeros. We lost no pilots that day.

Above: **Much of the early air fighting from Guadalcanal was shared by US Navy and Marine pilots. Navy Wildcats, F4Fs, were a common sight on Henderson Field.**
/Grumman Aircraft

Right: **Bell P-39s and P-400s—the latter being essentially a P-39 with the more reliable 20mm cannon than the 37mm gun fitted to the former—also fought in the Solomons beside the Warhawks.**

Right: White-tailed
Warhawks of the 44th FS on
Munda Airfield. Led by Maj
Kermit Tyler and Maj John
Little, the 44th downed $111\frac{1}{2}$
enemy aircraft in exchange
for eight of its own pilots lost
between July and September
1943./*USAF*

Below: First P-40N-5 of the
45th FS, 15th FG, lands on
Baker Island, September
1943./*USAF*

Below: A 44th FS Warhawk
lands on Munda Airfield,
New Georgia, 14 August,
1943./*USAF*

Left: The 45th FS's Warhawks were painted overall 'sand', very close to the 'sand' in the RAF 'sand and spinach', or as one pilot described it to us, '... about the colour of good ol' Georgia red clay.'/*USAF*

Below left: The Japanese Betty bomber was a Navy G4M1-3 built by Mitsubishi and operated widely in the Pacific, including the Solomons./*USAF*

Bottom left: By early December 1943, the 45th FS had moved to Nanumea Island in the Ellice Islands, east of the Solomons, presumably to make sure that the enemy did not slip in the Allies' back door./*USAF*

Appendices

1

P-40 Data

	P-40 Tomahawk Mk I[1] H81-A/A-1	P-40B Tomahawk Mk 11A H81-A2	P-40C Tomahawk Mk IIB H81-A3	P-40D Kittyhawk Mk I H87-A2
Empty weight	5,376lb	5,590lb	5,812lb	6,208lb
Maximum weight	7,215lb	7,645lb	8,058lb	8,809lb
Wing span	37ft 4in	37ft 4in	37ft 4in	37ft 4in
Wing area	236sq ft	236sq ft	236sq ft	236sq ft
Length	31ft 8½in	31ft 8½in	31ft 8½in	31ft 2in
Tread	8ft 2in	8ft 2in	8ft 2in	8ft 2in
Maximum speed[2]	357mph	352mph	345mph	350mph
Normal cruise	277mph	273mph	270mph	298mph
Landing speed	80mph	80mph	85mph	84mph
Normal range	770 miles	730 miles	730 miles	800 miles
Service ceiling	32,750ft	32,500ft	29,500ft	30,600ft
Initial climb	3,080ft/min	2,860ft/min	2,650ft/min	2,580ft/min
Fuel capacity (internal)	160gal	160gal	160gal	148gal

Below: **Converted to a two-place fighter trainer this P-40E became a P-40ES.** */US Army*

Notes
(1) Tomahawk IA and IB same as Mk I except for radio and instruments
(2) At 15,000ft

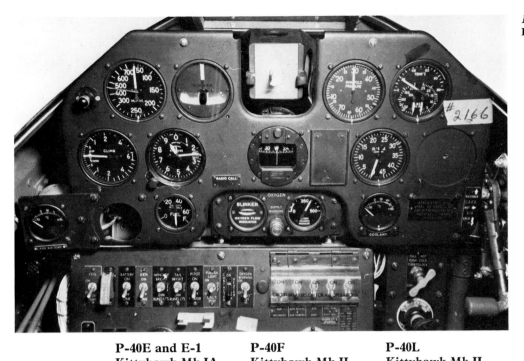

#2166

	P-40E and E-1 **Kittyhawk Mk IA** **H87-A3 and A-4**	**P-40F** **Kittyhawk Mk II** **H87-B3**	**P-40L** **Kittyhawk Mk II** **H87-B4**
Empty weight	6,350lb	6,590lb	6,150/6,340lb
Maximum weight	9,200lb	9,350lb (w/aux tank 9,870lb	9,000/9,100lb
Wing span	37ft 4in	37ft 4in	37ft 4in
Wing area	236sq ft	236sq ft	236sq ft
Length	31ft 2in	31ft 8½in (33ft 4in F-10 to F-20 inc)	31ft 8½in (33ft 4in L-5 to L-20 inc)
Tread	8ft 2in	8ft 2in	8ft 2in
Maximum speed	354mph at 15,000ft	364mph at 20,000ft	370mph at 20,000ft
Normal cruise	300mph	290mph	295mph
Service ceiling	29,000ft	34,400ft	36,000ft
Initial climb	2,050ft/min	3,250ft/min	3,300ft/min
Fuel capacity (internal)	157gal	157gal	127gal

	P-40K[3] **Kittyhawk Mk III**	**P-40M** **Kittyhawk Mk III**	**P-40N** **Kittyhawk Mk IV**
Empty weight	6,400lb	5,454lb	6,000lb (N-1) 6,200lb (N-5 to N-40 inc)
Maximum weight	10,000lb	8,900lb	8,850lb
Wing span	37ft 4in	37ft 4in	37ft 4in
Wing area	236sq ft	236sq ft	236sq ft
Length	31ft 8½in (K-1 and K-5) 33ft 4in (K-10 to K-15 inc)	33ft 4in	33ft 4in
Tread	8ft 2in	8ft 2in	8ft 2in
Maximum speed	362mph at 15,000ft	360mph at 20,000ft	378mph at 10,000ft (N-5 to N-40 350mph at 16,400ft)
Normal cruise	290mph	290mph	305mph (N-1)
Landing speed	85mph	85mph	85mph
Normal range	700 miles	700 miles	750 miles
Service ceiling	28,000ft	30,000ft	38,000ft (N-1) 31,000ft (N-5 to N-40 inc)
Initial climb	2,000ft/min	2,050ft/min	2,120ft/min
Fuel capacity (internal)	157gal	157gal	158gal

Notes

(3) The Curtiss-Wright suffix designators appear to have been abandoned following the H87-B3 model

P-40H and P-40J models cancelled

2

P-40 Engines

The Allison engines that powered the P-40s had a bore of 5.5in and a stroke of 6in, resulting in 1,710cu in displacement. The compression ratio was 6.65 : 1, and the fuel required 100/130 octane. Engine oil was USAAF specification AN-VV-0-446a, grade 1120 for warm weather, and 1100 for winter operation. Maximum coolant temperature was 257°F; minimum take-off temperature 185°F, and normal operating temperature, 250°F.

The P-40s used six models of the Allison:

P-40, P-40B, P-40C V-1710-33, 930hp, 2,600rpm, 12,800ft
P-40D, P-40E, E-1 V-1710-39, 1,000hp, 2,600rpm, 10,800ft
P-40K V-1710-73, 1,000hp, 2,600rpm, 10,800ft
P-40M, P-40N V-1710-81, 995hp, 2,600rpm, 15,700ft
P-40N V-1710-99, 955hp, 2,600rpm, 15,700ft
P-40N V-1710-115, 955hp, 2,600rpm, 15,700ft
Normal cruise fuel consumption (75% power), 65–75gal/hr

The R-R Merlin 28, V-1650-1, which powered the P-40F and P-40L, was built by Packard in the US and was approximately 175lb heavier than the Allison. The Allisons ranged from 1,310lb to 1,385lb; the Merlin was 1,520lb dry. The Merlin, however, produced 1,010hp at 2,650rpm at 16,000ft. This engine possessed a single-stage, two-speed geared supercharger with ratios of 8.151 : 1, and 9.490 : 1. Cylinder bore was 5in and stroke 6in, giving a displacement of 1,649cu in.

P-36/P-40 Production

The RAF Mohawks (P-36s) were aircraft originally ordered by France. France had taken delivery of 200 H75-A1s and H75-A2s (export versions of the US Air Corps' P-36A and P-36B) from December 1938 to July 1939. The French then ordered 135 H75-A3s and 395 H75-A4s.

Between 20 and 25 A3s reached France. Between 35 and 40 A3s, in transit when France fell, were diverted to the French in north-west Africa. The balance of this 135-machine order, between 65 and 70 aircraft, were accepted by the RAF and designated Mohawk IIIs.

Only six H75-A4s reached France before the French surrender in May 1940. Another 23 were diverted to Martinique. Then, since a total of 174 actually had been built of this 395-machine order, the remainder, or 145 aircraft, plus 110 additional ones, or 255 in all, were taken by the RAF as Mohawk IVs. The RAF retained 166 of these machines in Britain for use as fighter trainers, and sent the rest to India and South Africa.

The RAF obtained an additional five H75-A5s from Hindustan Aircraft Ltd, which assembled them under licence in Mysore, India. These craft, along with 10 H75-A9s, captured in their crates by the British in Iran, saw service in India.

About 50 of the RAF Mohawk IIIs were given serial numbers beginning with AR630. The remaining 20 were serialed BK569–BK588.

The 166 Mohawk IVs retained in Britain were given the following RAF serials: BD918–BD979 (62); BJ434–BJ453 (20); BJ531–BJ550 (20); BJ574–BJ588 (15); BK876–BK879 (4); BL220–BL223 (4); BS730–BS742 (13); BS784–BS798 (15); BT470–BT472 (3); LA157–LA161 (5); plus five aircraft with serials in the AR680 or AR690 range.

Twenty H75-A7s, c/n 14424–14443, went to the Netherlands East Indies in May 1940 and saw combat there. The A7 version was powered with the Wright Cyclone R-1820-G205A engine of 1,100hp, was fitted with four wing-mounted 12.7mm Browning machine guns, and was billed by Curtiss-Wright at $31,676 less engine.

Apparently no accurate count exists of the fixed-gear H75 Hawks flown by the Chinese against the Japanese from late 1937 through 1940. The Curtiss-Wright 'Aircraft Billing' record lists only the 32 machines which were exported to China from the US. However, the Central Aircraft Manufacturing Corporation – originally set up in China by Curtiss-Wright, but later apparently operated by Generalissimo Chiang Kai-shek, with perhaps an American partner – purchased materials kits for 50 H75-Ms. Therefore, Chiang's forces probably operated as many as 80 such machines. Gen Claire Chennault said in his book (*The Way of a Fighter*; G. P. Putnam's Sons, NYC, 1949) only that he had 'three squadrons' of H75 Hawks.

USAAF P-40s

A total of 13,737 P-40s were built, more than half of which went to American Allies. Most of those sent to Great Britain, and all of those sent to Russia, were delivered with USAAF serial numbers. Therefore, although aircraft sent to Britain under provisions of the Lend-Lease Act are listed separately, they are included in the USAAF deliveries below. The P-40B/Tomahawk cost $60,562 (complete) in 1941, down to $44,892 in 1944 for the P-40N-40.

XP-40

Total produced 1
Serial 38-010; converted from 10th production P-36A. Delivered October, 1938.

P-40

Total produced 199
Serials 39-156–39-220; 39-222–39-289 and 40-292–40-357. Deliveries June–October 1940.

P-40G

Total produced 1
Serial 39-221. A P-40 fitted with export H81-A2 wings. An additional 44 P-40Gs resulted when original P-40s were retro-fitted with H81-A2 wings.

P-40B

Total produced 131
Serials 41-5205–41-5304, and 41-13297–41-13327. Deliveries January–April 1941.

P-40C

Total produced 193
Serials 41-13328–41-13520. Deliveries March–May 1941.

P-40D

Total produced 22
Serials 40-359, and 40-361–40-381. First of the H87 series. Deliveries July 1941.

XP-46

Total produced 2
Serials 40-3053 and 40-3054. Delivered September 1941.

P-40E

Total produced 820
Serials 40-358; 40-382–40-681; 41-5305–41-5744; 41-13521–41-13599. Deliveries August 1941–May 1942.

P-40E-1

Total produced 1,500
Serials 41-24766–41-25195, and 41-35874–41-36953. Deliveries December 1941–May 1942.

XP-40F

Total produced 1
Serial 40-360. No delivery date shown in Curtiss records.

P-40F

Total produced 699
Serials 41-13600–41-13695, and 41-13697–41-14299. Deliveries January–August 1942.

P-40F-5

Total produced 123
Serials 41-14300–41-14422; Long fuselage. Deliveries in August 1942.

P-40F-10

Total produced 127
Serials 41-14423–41-14599; Manual cowl flaps. Deliveries October and November 1942.

Left: **This two-place P-40 has a mirror system which enabled instructor to monitor instruments in front cockpit.** /*USAF*

P-40F-15

Total produced   200
Serials 41-19733–41-19932; Winterised.
Deliveries December 1942.

P-40F-20

Total produced   112
Serials 41-19933–41-20044; Demand oxygen system. Deliveries in January 1943.

P-40K-1

Total produced   600
Serials 42-45722–42-46321; Dorsal fin. Deliveries May–August 1942.

P-40K-5

Total produced   200
Serials 42-9730–42-9929; Delivered September 1942.

P-40K-10

Total produced   335
Serials 42-9930–42-10264; Long fuselage. Deliveries in October and November 1942.

P-40K-15

Total produced   165
Serials 42-10265–42-10429; Winterised. Deliveries November 1942.

P-40L-1

Total produced   50
Serials 42-10430–42-10479; Short fuselage, two guns per wing. Deliveries in January 1943.

P-40L-5

Total produced   220
Serials 42-10480–42-10699; Long fuselage. Deliveries in January and February 1943.

P-40L-10

Total produced   148
Serials 42-10700–42-10847; Armour removed from coolant tank. Deliveries February and March 1943.

P-40L-15

Total produced   112
Serials 42-10848–42-10959; Permanent carb air filter. Deliveries March and April 1943.

P-40L-20

Total produced   170
Serials 42-10960–42-11129; Improved radio. Deliveries in April 1943.

P-40M-1

Total produced   60
Serials 43-5403–43-5462; Carb air by-pass gill added rt/front cowl. Long fuselage and six guns. Deliveries in November 1942.

P-40M-5

Total produced   260
Serials 43-5464–43-5722; Permanent carb air filter. Deliveries November and December 1942.

P-40M-10

Total produced   280
Serials 43-5723–43-6002; Mechanical landing-gear indicator each wing. Deliveries January and February 1943.

P-40N-1

Total produced   400
Serials 42-104429–42-104828; Lightweight; four guns. Fastest Warhawk. Deliveries in March and April 1943.

P-40N-5

Total produced   1,100
Serials 42-104829–42-105928; Improved radio. Deliveries May–July 1943.

P-40N-10

Total produced   100
Serials 42-105929–42-106028; Winterised. Deliveries in August 1943.

P-40N-15

Total produced   377
Serials 42-106029–42-106405; Six guns restored. Delivery dates not given C-W records; probably September 1943.

P-40N-20

Total produced   1,523
Serials 42-106406–42-106428, and 43-22752–43-24251. New canopy with improved vision to rear. Six guns; three 500lb bombs. Deliveries September–December 1943.

P-40N-25

Total produced   499
Serials 43-24252–43-24570, and 43-24572–43-24751. Non-metal self-sealing tanks. Deliveries January and February 1944.

P-40N-30

Total produced   500
Serials 44-7001–44-7500. Minor accessory changes. Deliveries April–June 1944.

P-40N-35

Total produced   500
Serials 44-7501–44-8000. New radio and ADF. Deliveries July–September 1944.

P-40N-40

Total produced   216
Serials 44-47749–44-47964; 1,000 ordered but last 784 cancelled. Automatic boost and prop control. Deliveries October and November 1944.

XP-40Q
Total produced 1
Serial 43-24571. Three additional Qs were modified from P-40H-1 s/n 42-45722, and from P-40K-10s s/n 42-9987 and s/n 42-10219.

P-40R
Approximately 300 P-40Fs and Ls were re-fitted with Allison engines due to a shortage of parts for the Merlin. These craft were re-designated P-40R-1s (Fs), and P-40R-2s (Ls).

Total P-40s to USAAF   11,995
(includes Lend-Lease)
XP-46   2

Export H81 Models and Tomahawks

CHINA (AVG)
H81-A2
Total export   100
C-W c/n random from 15337 to 15972.

RAF s/n in the AM370 to AM519 block. Taken from an RAF order. Not Lend-Lease. Delivered for shipment to Universal Trading Corp January–March 1941.

GREAT BRITAIN
Tomahawk Mk I, Mk IA and Mk IB (H81-A1)
Total export   142
RAF s/n BK852, BK853; AH741–AH880. Not Lend-Lease. Deliveries September and October 1940.

Tomahawk Mk II and Mk IIA (H81-A2)
Total export   110
RAF s/n AH881–AH991. Two .50cal in nose; four .303cal in wings. Russia was given 24 of these machines. Deliveries October and November 1940.

Tomahawk Mk IIB (H81-A2 and 3)
Total export   828
RAF s/n AH992–AH999; AK100–AK570;

Below: **Soviet P-40E-1. Since the Russians received 2,091 P-40s, a very large part of the P-40 story remains untold. Russian P-40 squadron records are not available to Western researchers.**/*NASM*

AM370–AM519 (less 100 to AVG), and AN218–AN517. Four machines lost at sea; Russia received 49. Deliveries November 1940–August 1941.

Total Tomahawks to Britain 1,081
Total AVG Tomahawks 100
Total export Tomahawks 1,181

Export H87 Model Kittyhawks
GREAT BRITAIN

Kittyhawk Mk I (P-40D)
Total export 560
RAF s/n AK571–AK999 and AL100–AL230. Deliveries August–December 1941.

Kittyhawk Mk IA (P-40E and P-40E-1)
Total export 1,500
Previously counted under USAAF deliveries w/USAAF serials. RAF s/n ET100–ET999, and EV100–EV699. Lend-Lease. Deliveries September 1941–June 1942.

Kittyhawk Mk II (P-40F and P-40L)
Total export 230
Previously counted in USAAF deliveries. RAF s/n FL219–FL488. Delivered to RAF in July and August 1942. Lend-Lease.

Kittyhawk Mk III (P-40M-5 and M-10, P-40K)
Total export 364
Previously counted in USAAF deliveries. RAF s/n FR210–FR361; FR385–FR392; FR412–FR521, and FR779–FR872. Lend-Lease. Deliveries to RAF November 1942–January 1943.

Kittyhawk Mk IV (P-40N-1–P-40N-35 inc.)
Total export 458
Previously counted in USAAF deliveries. RAF s/n FR884, FR885; FT849–FT954, and FX498–FX847. Lend-Lease. Deliveries to RAF March 1943–January 1944.

RAF Kittyhawks from C-W 560
RAF Kittyhawks Lend-Lease 2,552

RUSSIA
The Soviets received 2,091 P-40s, various models, from the US. Britain transferred 94 Tomahawks and six Kittyhawks to the Russians. All of these aircraft are included in the USAAF totals given above.

Note: The Tomahawks and Kittyhawks flown by the Commonwealth Nations were supplied from RAF inventory.

Below: **Capt Walter Ohlrich, FEAF, HQ, at Nielson Field, Manila, Philippines, mid-1945. Late in the war, this P-40N was converted to two-place to give combat rides to ground support personnel. Ohlrich's crew chief declined a second such treat after Allied anti-aircraft gunners sent a round through the rear-seat canopy.**/*Walter Ohlrich, Jr*

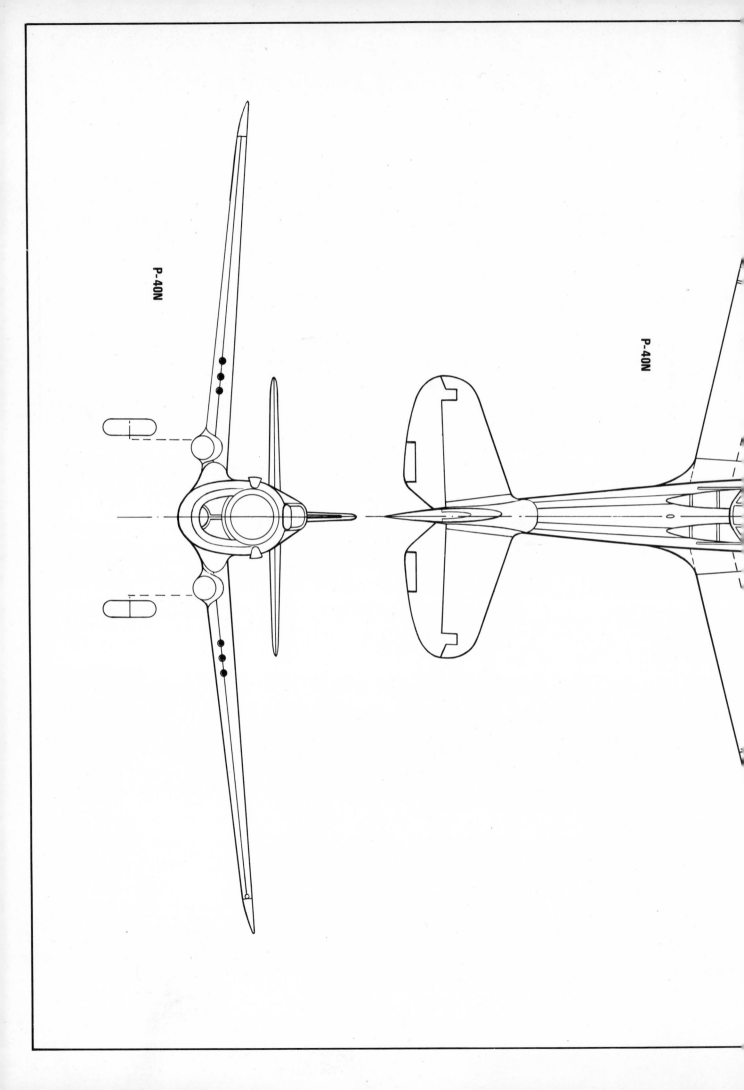

P-40N

P-40N